BREAKING
NORMAL

REWILD YOUR INNER CHILD
AND SET THE TRUTH FREE

Printed in the United States of America
ISBN: 978-0-9990564-1-7

BREAKING NORMAL

REWILD YOUR INNER CHILD AND SET THE TRUTH FREE

DANIEL EISENMAN

Contents

Acknowledgments

At this moment, I want to acknowledge you for listening to a comrade who decided to be led by something that wasn't normal and for being courageous enough to channel what that creative energy entailed. And it's happening right now. I acknowledge my divinely victorious daughter, Divina, who has affirmed an inkling I've had for a while. That inkling is that by surrendering to the energy of emotion that is flowing through us, we get to make the biggest impact in the world without trying. In her first month out of the womb, our connection inspired roughly a hundred million people in the world to consider a type of communication beyond words.

I acknowledge you, the reader, in that you are divinely guided.

I acknowledge the divinely brilliant, infinitely intelligent, unconditionally loving and unavoidably abundant energy that is living through me and everyone else that has ever existed. I acknowledge the Creator of the creator which is potentially un-nameable and for me the gap has been bridged with my REAL-

viii | *Daniel Eisenman*

ationship with Yeshua (aka Jesus) ~ even beyond religion. I acknowledge my parents for laying down a foundation of relating to other people with love as the number one lens to look through and go from there.

I acknowledge my queen bee (aka wife), Diana, for inspiring me to connect to God in ways I have never experienced prior to our communion. She is my inspiration in an infinite number of ways. To see her embrace the space between life & death and pleasure & pain while watching her birth our baby basically redefines my reality. That reality has been continuously refined and upgraded every time I have been able to gaze into the *YOUniverse* of her and my daughter's souls through their eyes. I am infinitely inspired, beyond words, to think about what that means to me. And this book, I trust, will serve as a guide to how I came to this connection and gratitude. I trust that it will serve as the most effective and efficient vehicle for catalyzing that in others in an even a greater way ... in my faith, it only gets better.

I acknowledge that place beyond time & space and beyond right & wrong and beyond words. I trust this book will serve as a peephole to where we can meet.

I acknowledge every one of my friends—some that are coming to my heart at the moment who are integral for this expression of **Breaking Normal** are JP Sears, Brandon Hawk, Perzan Irani, Eric Neff, Sel Kaya, Jill Renee Feeler, Frank Jay, Paul Risse, Tyson Wagner, and if I kept going, I could fill a whole library of books. I acknowledge you. You are no thing and you are everything and you are as you say you are. Thank you.

I acknowledge my immediate family, who are also my friends. Nathaniel and Emily, my brother and sister, I love you with all my heart. Timothy, my best friend, when I truly think about how thankful I am for you, tears seem to come before words. Mother, thank you for loving me, no matter what I do. And thank you to my father, for telling the truth even when it's weird. I am forever inspired how you two redefined your reality to protect and provide for me until I was ready for my own adventure.

I acknowledge my grandma who taught me that laughing till you cry or crying till you laugh is one of the healthiest forms of self-acceptance through self-expression. She also inspired me to let go of judging tears versus laughter or smiling versus frowning. She transitioned four days after 100 years of living. We now have Oriah, one of the puppies from Mema's dog.

I thank my dog, Oriah, for training me to become the best dad I can be. She has shown me the dynamic of what it means to be in a wolf pack and how the wellbeing of a tribe is dependent on good guidance from elders. She holds me accountable by reflecting where I'm at with my energy. She is one of the greatest catalysts I have ever had in understanding boundaries.

I acknowledge the sibling I never met. I acknowledge Bart Migom, the brother I never met in person. Bart and my sister were in love and he was highly inspired by and looking forward to meeting Diana and me. He was killed in the bombing at the Belgium airport on his way to the United States. I believe Bart was soulfully engaged until he was abruptly redirected into another dimension. Bart is a strong reminder that even when someone is following their heart we can never know where that may lead.

I am infinitely grateful for the midwife team who helped birth Divina and likewise for the team who helped birth this book: A very special man, who might be described as the archetype of the king magician, showed up in my life—Raj Lahoti—who blurs lines and breaks normal with the best of them; and Deborah Brown, who basically, in the book birthing world, would be a midwife; and for Sam Poppe who's been there from the start as a faithful scribe and truth follower.

This is holding me accountable to realize that the degree to which I can receive is probably the degree to which I can give, and everyone on this whole list has held me accountable to receiving so much greatness regardless of anything in return. Jah Bless.

I also want to acknowledge everyone who has invested time, money, faith, and presence into our experiences, our retreats, our videos, this book. It is so inspiring for people to come into my life and hold me accountable to be my best. These people have held a very sacred space at a high level of integrity for me to be fully seen and expressed and for me to fully show up because that is what they are doing. Thank you for holding that space for our co-evolution and for being my teachers.

Most people who have joined us for these experiences came for something they couldn't make sense of. Thanks for listening to an inkling, an intuitive call that is beyond practicality or what makes sense. Thanks for following that call, because I hear it too. And it's very affirming.

Foreword

I believe that the most dangerous liability in our world today is being yourself. Think about it: if you are being yourself, other people might find out who you really are, they might actually see you, and having seen you they might make fun of you, or reject you, or perhaps even worse, accept you. At the same time, by being yourself, you might actually see you, and who you see might be different than who you thought or who you wanted to see...

That's a scary proposition, and the best way to avoid it is by being normal.

At least, that's what our imaginations say. As ridiculous as that may sound, what's more ridiculous is how easily and how unconsciously we slip to behaviors that act that out. It's a fact that we all do it to some degree (and that fact is based on my delusional opinion). Being normal is one of the most pervasive diseases of our time, infecting 90% of people. The other 10% are infected too, they're just silent carriers. It's a disease, I believe, that is caused by a fear-based mindset of self-rejection. Though it is self-imposed, it also, in my experience, has roots in our childhoods.

One of the most fundamental human needs is the need for connection, and as kids this need is incredibly raw. Children and babies can actually die from failure to thrive syndrome if they don't have connection. And while there are many forms of connection, the one we learn early on is approval as the currency that gives us a sense of connection.

When Little JP felt approved of, he felt an experience of connection. So, he auditioned for Mommy and Daddy's approval, and when he got it, he felt like he mattered, like he belonged, like he was connected to others both physically and psychologically. I think we're all addicted to approval to one degree or another larger degree of it.

The easiest way to gain approval from someone is to please him or her. This is done not by being yourself, but by being like them, by mirroring the things they like about themselves, and suppressing the things they don't; it's done by reading the other person and becoming what he or she wants us to be.

I would bet that all of us experienced as kids times where we step fully into ourselves, where we went out on a limb in front of our parents or others, and were not only un-acknowledged, but were actually disapproved of. A very hot fire of shame that sends the message, "Don't touch the hot stove of Self again!"

That's how the disease can take root, and when it does the costs are steep. When normalcy becomes the religion we worship—we treat ourselves like the enemy. We reject ourselves because that ensures us no one else will have the chance to reject us. It's kind of like saying, "I'll just kill myself so that I don't die."

"Is there a cure for this disease," you're telepathically asking right now. Your own weirdness is the cure. While I'm not a doctor (unless I'm in denial) and that statement hasn't been evaluated by the FDA, or studied by NASA, I'd ask you to consider it anyway. Your weirdness is the cure—not someone else's.

What is weirdness? To me it's something too profound to be defined. So here's my definition anyway: weirdness is the traits, tendencies, behaviors and perspectives that help make you unique.

You might say, "JP, I'm just a boring normal person who wears a suit and pays my taxes on time." To your statement that you definitely just hypothetically said, I would say that you're in denial. You're far weirder than you think, you're probably weirder than you can think. If you challenge the person that lives inside your skin to observe yourself experiencing various aspects of the world, to listen to the things you choose not to say in certain situations, and hear the thoughts you don't pursue because they make no sense, to discover a wealth of weirdness within. That weirdness, I'd say, is a gluten-free breadcrumb trail that always leads you back to you, to your authentic self. I don't worship weirdness, but rather the place where weirdness leads—not to who you think you are, not to who you want to be, but to who you actually are.

Pretending for a moment that I know what the purpose of life is, I think it has to do with everyone—you, me, all of us—living our own life, giving ourselves permission to be the miracle that we are; expressing it, not hiding it. It's interesting how we all seem to say that this life we are given is precious, while wasting so much time and energy hiding ourselves from ourselves and other people.

And yet, when we think about the people who inspire us the most, it is never their normalcy that inspires us. No one has ever said, "Wow, I'm inspired by how well that guy exceeds at being normal." No, it's their weirdness. And not just their weirdness, but the way their weirdness delivers them to us, the way we get exposed to more of who they are, because they are willing to nonapologetically be themselves. They publicly risk being themselves, and that's inspiring. Perhaps we only get inspired by what we need.

So how do we bring our weirdness out? How do we slice through the psychological scar tissue of our collective programming that ensures we act normally, so that the miracle of who we are can actually arise?

In my experience, we don't need to go and "figure out" how to be weird, because beneath our clothes we're all naked weirdos. The cure, in that sense, is already inside of us. What is absolutely essential, though, is a willingness to embrace discomfort so that we can access our raw weirdness. Brené Brown says that he or she who is willing to be the most uncomfortable, is not only the bravest but rises the highest. If our friend Brené Brown is right, then part of us that doesn't want anything to change gets to say, "But embracing discomfort, feelings, and emotional pain might hurt us." I don't think anyone has ever been hurt by emotional pain, I think what hurts us is trying to avoid our pain and discomfort. While our survival instinct says pain is bad and we should move away from it, our self-realization instinct says pain is an opportunity and we should move towards it. There's meaning in pain, purpose in pain, and at the other side of pain, there's you. You are on the other side of pain because you are the one generating it.

Personally, I'm excited for the journey beyond normal that you're embarking on with Daniel. My excitement for your opportunity with this book is purely derived out of the gratitude I have for the abnormal impact Daniel has made on my career, life, and being. Daniel and I had a friendship at first sight encounter in February of 2013. In those early days, the best advice (and therefore the most irritating) that Daniel repeatedly shared with me was, "JP, you're playing it too safe." Because I'm a fast learner, he only had to tell me about 837 times before the message sunk in. A breakthrough began, or perhaps an upgraded statement, breaking normal began in my life. I began feeling and recognizing what I had been blind to, yet Daniel was able to see so clearly. I was protecting myself in a shell of normalcy so I could feel safe. My gifts, like the gifts of so many others, didn't match the fingerprint of normal and that was scary to me. It was great that it was finally scary to me, because that meant that I finally knew that I was in denial of them rather than being in denial of my denial of them. Now I could do something about it.

Over the next year and a half of our friendship, I found that the more I could embrace discomfort, the more I was breaking out of my self-induced prison of normalcy. The inspiration, friendship, and love that Daniel gave me always reassured me that discomfort is my friend, not my enemy. As I transitioned from interfacing with the world via my shell of safety to my unapologetic weird, authentic self, my peace and inner fulfillment skyrocketed. I was also shocked that the world seemed to embrace me more, the less I hid my authenticity. My willingness to let my weird perspectives, satirical humor, and caring heart out to play has generated more than 2 million fans on social media and over 250 million video views. Yet that all hinged on my willingness to be committed to breaking normal. Thank you, Daniel for being so bored with normal that you live in such an elevated way that everyone around you is inspired to embrace their version of weird.

In any given moment you have a choice. You can choose the cure for normal, which is saying an embodied "yes" to your weirdness. When you can say "yes" to your weirdness, you're more importantly living a "yes" to being you.

JP Sears

YouTube Sensation, Author, and Curious Student of Life

* * *

Author's Note: As I was putting finishing touches on this book, JP delivered a speech at a TEDx event in San Diego. I had arranged for JP to be among the speakers and I attended to support him. I arrived close to on time (read late) and miraculously scored front door parking. The door was already locked. Usually that's a deal breaker … again miraculously, they broke their rule and let me in. The applause for JP's introduction welcomed me into the room.

When JP finished, I turned to another friend and said, "I believe JP just wrote the Foreword to my book."

I am happy to see how the golden thread of JP's speech ties to his personal testimony about our REALationship.

Welcome

Countless people have attended or watched videos of the retreats facilitated by me and my tribe of like-hearted thought leaders. You may recognize me as a co-leader of the "RawBrahs" or as the co-founder of International Tribe Design. You may have seen me in a very special video that has gone around the world millions of times. I "om" a very special young lady to sleep, safe in the vibration she recognizes as her daddy's. See the video at *Facebook.com/danieleisenman*. Whatever has drawn you to me and my work, I am glad to have you here!

Over the past decade of creating epic retreats, I have traveled around the world experiencing the most beautiful settings and amazing people. I have picked at the golden threads and patterns of human interactions, using the environment to anchor all the learning going on (for me and the participants alike). I was able to discern some pretty important things in these ten years. One big observation is that many people keep the lid on their growth and personal development. This is a self-imposed limitation ... nobody tells us to do this!

Note to Self: *There is nothing wrong with you.*
Remember this as you read this book and do your life.

Breaking Normal: ReWild Your Inner Child and Set the Truth Free is your retreat experience in a book. You will get to feel what it means to be raw and vulnerable, excited and glowing with a sacred knowledge about your future. You'll also learn to communicate with others in a way that cuts through the limitations we used to let ourselves get entangled in. You will have tools and insight for building your own tribe, be it your family or community or the world at large.

If you hear the call to join us on one of our next Breaking Normal Experiences after reading this book, I trust I will see you there ... in the field ... beyond ... normal. I trust this book will serve as a vehicle for transformation, especially if you pour yourself into the exercises as if you were with me in person. We'll be together in spirit!

Aloha,
Daniel
BreakingNormal.com

Setting the Truth Free

As you proceed, please keep in heart that my personal exploration is not a new set of rules or dogma to follow. If you find any, break them. This is part of growth. If I listened to all the advice I was given about how I "should" write this book, there would be no book. Instead of taking out all the *funcomfortable* taboo topics and trying to mold this into the cookie cutter of a best seller, I trust the truth (even when it's weird) is what will serve us the best.

Although, many of the people's names have been modified, the stories that follow are based on real life experiences.

Please realize that I no longer facilitate some of the exercises in the same exact way, or at all (i.e., naked exercise) yet I kept it in the book for integrity to the true story.

Preface

Flashing red and blue lights in the rear view mirror. The sudden whoop of a police siren. All thirteen of us in the van stopped talking, and my brother Timothy, seated at the wheel, began to pull over.

"What's going on?" I asked him. "Were you speeding?"

"I don't know," Timothy responded, "I'm not even sure what the speed limit is."

It was late, almost midnight on the narrow winding road. We were driving out of Yellowstone National Park, feeling tired and hungry from a day spent in nature, and very much looking forward to getting back to the retreat house, where we would eat dinner and perhaps get one last exercise in before bed. The van was quiet, cozy. Some people in our group were nodding off, others were talking quietly.

Everyone woke up real quick when the cop pulled in behind us, and as we turned around to look out the back windows, a blinding spotlight hit us in the face. The interior of our van, all lit up now, suddenly felt more cramped than it did before.

There's something about cops that seems to put people on edge, as though the spotlight were an accusation rather than a standard safety procedure. The knee-jerk reaction is to check oneself, to pat one's pockets, scan the immediate vicinity and try to remember everything one has done in the past five minutes.

The silence in the van broke as people started to speculate and ask questions. One member of the group told a story about a past police run-in, which sparked someone else to relate a similar story, which reminded yet another member about her friend, or a friend of her friend, who had something bad happen to her, and the reason was *x* which meant we should do *y*. And so on. Improbable, and to me exaggerated, notions, simply by being spoken aloud, were repeated, taken seriously, and given traction. "Maybe we hit something. Maybe we swerved. Maybe they think we're drug dealers." The last comment, part-kidding, part-serious, about our vehicle, a white oversized conversion van with black tinted windows, earned a few laughs, and then other jokes were made. After that it seemed everyone was talking and it got louder in the van until someone in the back shouted for silence.

For a moment I felt similarly triggered, and noticed my heart beating faster, my armpits sweating. I remembered that I had a small amount of cannabis in my bag, which wouldn't have worried me if had we been in California, where I am medically registered, but we weren't, and I briefly considered swallowing it. An older version of myself might have done so, but now, sitting in the van, I decided that if the officer asks, I would tell him the truth. I reminded myself to breathe, because while my mind could spin out numerous stories to explain and frame the encounter we were about to have, I didn't know what was happening, and neither, it seemed, did anyone else in our group. So instead of letting the stories run away with me, by resisting or engaging them, I chose instead to notice and observe them while focusing a bit more on the sensations in my body.

In general, there are four reactions to physical and emotional stress: fight, flight, freeze and façade. All four were on display, in the form of defensiveness, excuse making, shutting down, and downplaying.

The cop walked around our vehicle, flashlight in hand, inspecting every inch.

Timothy rolled down the driver-side window.

"License and registration. Do you know why I pulled you over? We clocked you at fifty-seven back there. The speed limit is forty-five."

The cop walked around to the passenger side, opened the door, and poked his head inside. The person seated closest to that door was Terrell, the only black person in our group. When the cop asked him to step out of the vehicle, panic ensued.

"Whoa whoa whoa" someone said from the back. "What's going on? Why does he have to step out? What's the reason for this?"

"It's all right," the cop responded. "I just have to ask him a few questions."

More than one person in our group pulled out their cell phone thinking they were about they thought they were about to witness the next viral episode of perceived police injustice. The spotlight, however, made it impossible to see what was happening. A litany of speculation erupted, with all four stress responses again running rampant.

A few minutes later the two returned, and the cop asked Amy, another member of our group, to please step out. When they departed, Terrell was bombarded with questions.

"I told him we were here for a retreat," he began. "Practicing honesty and self-expression, but I don't think he believed me." When the cop came back with Amy, I imagined from his facial expression that he was confused and possibly frustrated. With barely a word, he pulled out a third person, Kyle.

None of us knew how much time had passed, nor what we'd done to warrant the extra questioning, but it was clear the officer suspected us of more than speeding. Outside we heard Kyle and the officer raise their voices, and when they returned to the van, Kyle seemed rattled. The cop told us to hang tight.

"He got in my face," Kyle reported, "actually got in my face. I told him we're here for a retreat, focusing on health and freedom through raw honesty, and he told me I was lying. Then I pulled my phone out and began videotaping and that's when everything escalated."

"I told the same thing," Amy added, "and he looked at me like I was crazy."

Sometime later the cop's partner or superior arrived, and this guy seemed more cordial and apologized for the delay, explaining that, while we were pulled over for speeding, there was another infraction for which we were being investigated. He then asked for our names and phone numbers while his colleague pulled out another suspect. One member of our group refused to provide the information, which created some tension in me and, I imagine, in the rest of the group as well.

Right up until we got pulled over, we had a plan for how the rest of our night was going to go. The moment those flashing lights went on, however, the plan changed, and got further and further away with every passing minute. Rather than accepting that change of plan and co-creating a new one, some members of our group seemed resentful for the interruption, and wanted it to be over as quickly as possible, and that resistance seemed to make the encounter longer and less pleasant.

"Have you seen any wolves around here?" I asked the superior.

"Wolves?"

Yea, I've been in the park a handful of times over the past month, and I've seen a lot of wildlife, but not any wolves, which is something I was desiring to see—from a safe distance."

"Oh sure," he answered, and went on to say that most likely, at that very moment, there was one within a mile radius of us, watching. He sees them all the time, he said, usually at night on patrol.

The partner came back and pulled someone else out of the van, and a few minutes later, another. The whole encounter by now was getting long and drawn out and people's irritation was starting to show. Not only were they *hangry*, but many of them had paid a lot of money to come on this retreat, expecting me and Timothy to deliver a life-changing experience, and to them this police interaction might have seemed like a total distraction.

I, on the other, was excited to be pulled over by the police, and grateful for the opportunity. Whenever our retreats intersect with the so-called *real world*, it's a chance to put into practice the things we talk about, to walk the talk and remain open through potentially challenging encounters. So not only was I not afraid of being questioned, I was anxious to get the chance. When the partner came back for another suspect, in fact, I actually leaned forward with the intention of getting picked. It was obvious that the officers had sort of assumption or suspicion against us, just like some people in the van had assumptions and suspicions against them, but I wanted to dial it back further and stick to what had happened. If it was true that we had indeed committed some infraction other than speeding, I wanted to know what it was so that we could make amends and move forward, possibly learning something in the process. In my mind, the police intervention was divinely conceived, our paths crossing for a reason, and though the encounter might have felt hostile at times, ultimately, I had faith that we were on an even bigger team, the Human Team, and therefore, despite the apparent differences between me and the officers, their uniforms as compared to my flip flops, for example, the similarities were far greater. I trusted from experience that the more I opened up, the more they might too, and that the things we both considered to be deeply personal were actually universal.

Then it happened. Having figured out by now who among our group was in charge, the cops asked me and Timothy to step out.

"Ok" he began, "we've been hearing a lot of stories from your colleagues, a lot of new-agey, hippie-dippie type of stuff. I understand that you two are running a retreat and that it has something to do with health and honesty, though I'm not sure what, and quite frankly, it sounds suspicious."

I caught myself in the act of crossing my arms, which is a closed off, defensive position, like a wolf raising its hackles, so before I answered, and because it's cold out, I shook them out a little, put my hands in my pockets, and rocked slightly on my feet as a way of staying loose.

"We run retreats," I said, "about breaking normal, hacking the rat race, and upgrading the matrix. We get *funcomfortable* and practice *REALlationships*, moving beyond a reliance on agreement-based connections. We get people out of their heads and into their hearts, and teach self-acceptance through self-expression to help them gain clarity and freedom in their lives. It's health…through honesty."

They both looked at us for a long moment.

"Ok," the officer said, waving his hand dismissively, "we're going to ask you some questions now, and the best course of action for you is to be honest and tell the truth.

I smiled. "Great, that's exactly what I do."

Introduction

What are these retreats about?

It's a common question, one I get asked by a lot of the people who reach out to me after they've seen my videos on social media. They want to know what the retreats are about so that they can decide whether they should explore further. People ask, because even though they might be busy or skeptical, they're also curious, feel an inkling or feel called to attend. Before they make the investment— of time and money and logistics and the potential for change—they want to know ahead of time that it will be worth it.

Some of the most significant aspects of my life, though, came from the things I couldn't possibly have "assessed" ahead of time—things that made my heart beat faster, a sensation I may have interpreted as excitement or nervousness—on which I took a leap of faith: getting married, starting a family, continuing on a non-traditional career path, my friends and business partnerships.

The people who ask me that question usually want the basics, which is a fun challenge for me because of all the weird and wonderful and miraculous things I've experienced on the retreats.

Finding the love of their life and quitting their unfulfilling jobs … coming out of the closet in more ways than one, serious amounts of weight loss. Or a midnight polar plunge with fluorescent plankton in British Columbia. Or impromptu performances I've seen otherwise shy and reserved people suddenly put on. Every retreat is different, with different people, in different moments in time.

With all that said, while I may not be able to answer whether a specific retreat will be worth it, I can say that in my experience, following the call, one's beating heart, is more than worth it.

Think of the retreats as long weekends, where you go away from where you currently live, away from the people you know, your friends, family, coworkers, and acquaintances. You drive or fly or take a boat or train or bus or hitchhike and then you get here—to a location on Earth that we've chosen for the rawness and beauty of its nature. In the past that's been Yellowstone National Park, with its geysers and wildlife and mountain lakes and springs; it's been a private island off the coast of Panama, with forests in the clouds; it's been Hawaii with its remoteness in the ocean, clear night skies, and ancient volcanoes: one of them in particular, Haleakala, has a massive crater that is alleged to be the quietest place on earth. We've been to high altitude lakes in Steamboat Springs, Colorado, where we were surrounded by wildlife, by animals doing what animals are prone to do, which is be themselves; we've been to one of the oldest forests in the world, outside Byron Bay, Australia, where we hiked among trees many hundreds of years old; we've been skiing in Utah and cliff diving in Kauai. Costa Rica has been a repeat location, not only for its stunning nature, but also for the way the residents and culture interact with the land. Perhaps that's why it's consistently ranked at the top of the Happy Planet index, which measures a country's happiness, ecological impact, and sustainable well-being. Whatever the location, that's what we're looking for: biodynamic places where we can see the Earth's natural forces being exerted and absorbed and expressed in harmonious ways, which is then a reflection of what we do on retreats—celebrate and align with our individual natures, rather than fear them or conceal them or bottle them up. For some, that aligning might start with acknowledging and accepting the ways in which one isn't aligned. If that's where you're currently at, then that's a great place to start.

Then there's the people you'll meet when you arrive, anywhere from three to a hundred-plus, some who will seem to be like you, and others who won't. They too have come from somewhere else, having left their homes, friends, and families.

What brings people to the retreat is unique for everyone. A commonality I have noticed is the desire for something new, something different, something more—those old feelings that seem to have been with us through almost all of human history. This is not true in everyone at every moment, necessarily; it's more like a torch that is passed on through time.

Since you're reading this, I imagine the torch has been passed to you.

Like the other attendees, you arrive at the retreat without quite knowing what to expect, and that in itself is part of the process, not being overly attached to specific outcomes. How do you know if you're overly attached? I would say if things don't go according to your plan and you notice yourself becoming ungrounded or acting in ways you might feel not so stoked about afterwards, that could be a sign. On the other hand, if you can observe things unfolding however they unfold, and if you can accept that unfolding while at the same time accepting the part of yourself that wanted to plan in the first place, and the part of yourself that has something valuable to contribute, you are in the sweet spot of this retreat.

And then we play. I don't know of a better word to encapsulate what it is we do. We play in nature. We experiment with the types of things that we might have had the gusto to try as kids. We play observation games and truth-telling games and inspiration games. We explore and breathe and relax and be who we are at any given moment. We seek out the people at the retreat who we initially thought were weird, or different from us because those people may start to attract us, and while in our former lives we might not have been willing or able to approach such a person based solely on a hunch with almost no words to back it up, here we can, and do. We ask them a question we might never ask in any other context: *What do you really think? What's going on with you at this moment? What reality are you living in? What story are you telling yourself?*

The transience of our connection also quickens it.

Amazing things happen, as you'll also see in the coming chapters. People break down. They break through. They break into song and dance. There's been flooding, there's been fighting, there's been moments of pure collective bliss.

My intention in writing this book is for it to be as much like a retreat as possible, and to impart some measure of the experience. It's not to bombard you with information, or tell you anything you should do, or need to do, but simply to share some of the things that we do, the things we talk about and think about, me and the hundreds of other people who come on retreats, the hundreds of friends I've met and made because of these practices and exercises and experiences. I don't know how to explain it, and I'm not sure that I want to, but after dozens of retreats, all I can say is that they're miraculous, and in this day and age, *healing*.

Then there's this, perhaps the thing I most desire for you to get out of this book: What happens in these pages need not be limited to a one-weekend retreat. It can become a lifestyle.

What's most personal
is most universal.

Chapter 1

Original Sin

Why did Adam and Eve get kicked out of the Garden of Eden? Perhaps for the same reason we did: *listening to the serpent rather than God.*

Before that moment they lived naked, unashamed, and in harmony with the world around them. Along came the serpent, however, which slithered up and whispered in Eve's ear, "You see that tree over there? You should eat its fruit. It will give you special knowledge."

Eve told Adam and the two of them got to thinking, maybe we should...and acting against the will of God, they did.

Unless you're a *Parselmouth*, it's not an actual snake. Instead it's a friend, a parent, a preacher, teacher, coach, or bully. It's a commercial on TV, an item in a store, a YouTube video, a Facebook post, a digitally enhanced Instagram picture, even a book...perhaps even this book, depending on your interpretation. These are all potential serpents, some subtle, some not so subtle. They whisper in your ear about what you should and shouldn't do. They shout and advertise about what you should buy. They "advise" you about what your job or career should be, what you're good at and what you're not. They tell you how you should look and act. "You're not enough," they say, "you're too much, you're this, you're that." And so on. "Unless you do x, y, or z."

In short, they're *shoulding* on you. When you start listening and believing what they say, you *should* on yourself. That, in a coconut shell, is how you get banished from the Garden. That is how a heavenly life can feel like a living hell.

Perhaps this is the essence of Original Sin, sin meaning to act without God.

I believe that we are all creations of the Creator, endowed with the divine and universal energy. The light within me is the same light within you, within everyone else and everything else. We are like individual light bulbs connected back to the same source, and yet, no two bulbs are exactly the same. We come in different colors, sizes and shapes, with different perspectives, ideas and dreams. Those variables make the light shine through us in a very particular way, and it wants to shine through us in that particular way, otherwise we wouldn't be here. Our job as light bulbs is to shine.

As kids we knew what that meant. Rather, we didn't "know," didn't have to think about it. We did it. Like Adam and Eve, we were born naked and unashamed and raw and spontaneous and real. Bundles of energy, acutely sensitive, radically alive. We glowed with the flow and acted the way we felt. We didn't filter ourselves; the delay from impulse to expression was *physiological*, not *psychological*.

Everything was new, and we lived at the surface of our skin. If something looked strange, we asked about it. If it was appealing, we went for it. We played, we explored, we expressed. Nothing we did brought about reproach, because to the adults watching us we were innocent, and everything we did was cute, brilliant, and miraculous. We pooped, peed, picked our noses, farted, rolled over, played dead, laughed, screamed, sang, cried, imitated others, pretended to be kings or queens or bandits, and played with our food at the dinner table. We allowed at all times, as Whitman says, "nature to speak without check with original energy."

At some point in our young lives, however, a shadow may have appeared. We looked up, squinted our eyes to make out what it was, and more often than not saw a parent or authority figure hovering over us. Suddenly, without reason (or without reason we could understand), something we were doing, something we'd done many times, suddenly that thing was no longer ok. Suddenly that thing was bad. And we had better stop doing that something (stop doing it in public at least) or risk punishment, which may have felt like a fall from grace and a loss of love. The message, which from our perspective was arbitrary and probably unfair, was essentially, "You're too much. Your light is too bright, too dim, or odd colored, etc."

This is the first shutting down, so far back in our individual and collective memory as to pass into myth. Before that moment there was no history, only the eternal, ever-present now. After that moment, a story of repressed emotions is birthed.

***

As adults, many people tend to minimize and downplay the impact of such experiences. Such "corrective" punishment seems like a micro-incident that kids should easily get over, which is to say, put in perspective. We forget that kids don't have the same perspective as adults. They're three, four, maybe five years old. Or younger. To a kid the incident is not micro, but macro. It's earth-shattering, probably the biggest thing that happens that day.

Imagine being small and relatively powerless in relation to the giants around you. Imagine the warmth that comes from love, and the cold that comes from punishment. It must be confusing for kids when one moment the sun is shining, and the next moment, for reasons one might not understand, it's blotted out. This kind of confusion is what prompted ancient peoples to perform various sacrifices during solar eclipses, because they thought the gods were displeased. Imagine their confusion when the world went dark, and the relief and joy at seeing the sun again. Maybe they thought their sacrifice pleased the gods, and learned in the future to make regular sacrifices to keep their place in the sun.

In the modern age there might not be literal, ritualistic sacrifices, but cultures do exist that promote partial sacrifice in the form of social conformity. You can simply go to a playground to see it happen. Look how alive the kids are, how they seem to be bursting with energy. Then watch what happens when one of the kids gets in trouble, when he or she falls from parental favor. A lot of times the child is isolated, scolded, and sent to timeout, which mirrors the way we incarcerate adults. Watch the body language, the facial expression of that child. He looks confused, angry, and above all, ashamed. He sits in timeout and barely moves, barely breathes. The world has temporarily ended. Actually, energetically, he might think he has ended, while his friends continue to play without him. When the parents release him from purgatory, he's saved. He leaps up ecstatically—that is, until he remembers, and that's the crucial moment: he checks himself, tempers his excitement, and reenters the playground.

It's easy as adults to shrug this off. "So what? He acted out of line and the parent taught him a lesson." On the one hand that's true, the parent's intention was to correct a very specific behavior, and the child's "self-modification" is seen as evidence of learning. On the other hand, the lesson that gets through, especially the first few times it is "taught" is usually deeper, more jarring: not that a certain behavior is bad, but that the child is bad, no longer pure and innocent and good. That's the fall, when a child learns that there is "evil" inside him or her, certain urges and tendencies that are gross or wrong. The warmth of acceptance is contrasted with the cold of exclusion, and one learns from that point forward to repress the bad and express the good, and thereby keep one's place in the sun.

The challenge, however, is that no one comes into the world feeling evil, wrong, or gross. That's a learned behavior, learned from the sting of other people's reactions. There's no way to know, in the moment before expression, whether the thing one wants to express will be well-received by others. Childhood, then, can turn into a sort of guessing game, where wrong guesses bring about shame and repression, and right guesses bring about praise.

Kids are often told to be honest and tell the truth. At some point in the course of growing up, however, many learn that the adults telling them to tell the truth don't really mean it, or don't mean "the whole truth." Some kids get punished for being "too honest," and when that happens, like the biblical Fall, there seems to be forever after a shadow in our consciousness. From that point on, they are aware of two truths in every situation: the inner and the outer. It often happens that rewards and punishments alike stem from how well one obeys the outer truth to the detriment and disregard of the inner one. In school, for example, kids learn not only spelling, grammar, and arithmetic, but also how to please the teacher, how to raise their hands and come up with the "right" answer. Socially, many make friends and fit in first by mimicking and later by adopting the approved behaviors and lingo. It becomes safer, over time, not to be one's self, because what if that self gets rejected? Instead one acts out a version, a fraction of his or her full self. Rather than feeling their way through life, they think their way around it, trying to control the future by playing other people, anticipating what they want, and tailoring themselves accordingly.

In short, out of the desire for acceptance and the concern for what others might think, a lot of people growing up consciously or subconsciously dim their light in the presence of others, essentially sending a message to the Creator wishing they were different than they actually are.

To me that sounds a lot like worshiping someone else's opinion rather than honoring who and what we are. The result of such worship over time, if we continually suppress our thoughts and feelings, is that we may lose touch with those thoughts and feelings. We lose self-confidence, that is, confidence in ourselves. Serpents of all kind can slither up and whisper in our ear, tempting us off our path, leading us step by step, tongue-bite by tongue-bite, out of the Garden. Fast forward ten, twenty, thirty years, and we might end up lost, or as Alan Watts says it, at the top of a ladder, only to discover that it's leaning against the wrong wall. That's when another story, possibly the biggest delusion of all, rears its head. "That's life. That's the way things are, it was never about achieving dreams, but about learning to give them up…"

***

All that is in the past, and whatever happened happened for a divine reason. It is possible to recover the spirit of our inner child, and to nurture that spirit with the consciousness of an adult. Some refer to this as "The Hero's Journey," a coming home. The goal is to move beyond the "why, because" games, to stop arguing for our limitations and start asking ourselves what we truly desire and how we can achieve it.

When you shift the conversation, both internally and externally, to "what" and "how" rather than "why, because," you activate a new set of muscles. You start to co-create life rather than manage it. You no longer nip your ideas and inspirations in the bud because they don't seem practical or possible. Instead you focus on what you value. You let go of practicality for a while, and begin to think beyond the limits. Is this thing desirable? Is this what I or we want? If so, let's do it. Let's figure out how to do it.

As soon as the fruit hit their lips, Adam and Eve felt shame. Shame, because in their heart of hearts they knew better. They knew that eating the fruit was an act of betrayal against their higher nature, their Creator and God. In their shame, they covered themselves up with fig leaves and tried to hide in a grove. God found them, of course, found them out, because the heart always knows. I believe we know better too.

If the beginning of shame marks the end of feeling, the beginning of feeling can mark the end of shame. Shame led us out of the Garden, but it can, paradoxically, lead us back in. You can't think your way around it, though. You must feel your way through.

That's how we rewild the inner child and set the truth free.

I agree to love beyond
agreement.

Chapter 2

Agreements

We start the retreats with a set of agreements, intended to establish trust within the group, laying the framework for everything that follows.

Keep in mind that these aren't mandatory. No one has to agree to any or all of them, and the only thing that will happen if they don't is that they might be asked to sit out some exercises, for reasons I trust will become clear.

With that said, I believe the best way to ensure having the fullest retreat-experience possible is to take these agreements to heart, at least for the weekend, and to do one's best to honor them, and be open to talking about it either way.

***

The first agreement is to *tell the truth*.

What this means for me is honoring myself enough to share the things I think and feel with other people. Not only answering questions as honestly as possible, but also, and perhaps more importantly, expressing the things that, when they come up in me, are combined with sensations like an elevated heartbeat, flushed cheeks, jittery limbs, etc. Those types of symptoms—which I interpret as feelings of aliveness—are for me a clue that the thing I may not want to share, is the very thing from which I have a lot to gain by sharing. I've heard it said that a person is only as sick as his or her secret, and to me that means the things I hold in out of fear might actually have a hold over me, and the way to liberate myself from that hold is to share those things, to let go, and release into peace.

There's a guy named Brad Blanton, who is a doctor, pioneering psychotherapist, and the author, among other books, of *Radical Honesty*. During his career of treating patients, he came to see that lying was the single greatest cause of stress and unhappiness in their lives. By lying he means specially withholding, that is, not saying certain things to oneself or other people out of fear as to how they will react.

This idea has been a major influence on me. What's interesting is that people can be afraid of a reaction that hasn't even taken place yet, a reaction that they don't really know for sure will happen. So, it's not even the actual reaction they are afraid of, but rather their own imagination of how someone else will react. I believe that if someone chooses to act on that fear he or she is potentially practicing being in fear, instead of being led by faith.

Consider this for a moment: they're worshiping their own imagination rather than the reality of the other person; they're denying the other person's integrity by assuming they know how he or she will respond to what they have to say. In a deep sense, they're presuming to exercise some sort of control over another person.

A common rebuttal I hear at this point is, "Daniel, I can't be honest in my daily life because the people I live with (my mom or dad or girlfriend or grandma) aren't willing to go there with me. When I hear that, what I really hear is, "Daniel, I can't be honest in my daily life because I can't handle myself when people react to my truth." Which is not the same thing. The reason I have people in my life who are willing to go there with me is because I am willing to go there first. Or, as my brother puts it, "It takes two people to have a shallow conversation."

Here's what this agreement is not: a permission slip to go out and say all the negative things you might think about someone else. *"You're fat. You're stupid. You're ugly. You're gross."* That's not telling the truth. That's projecting your own insecurities onto someone else and saying that it's theirs.

Here's what this agreement is: a container, or a context, that we as a tribe or family or group of friends are willing to enter into so that we can live inside-out and speak about things as they come up; an invitation to share what you might not want to share, and to allow yourself to be seen for who you are in any given moment, in your rawness, rather than with the "normal" mask or script you might have been accustomed to in the past.

***

The second agreement is to *hear the truth*.

If we're going to tell our truth, and we want people to listen, we probably ought to be willing to do the same thing in return. Implicit in the Golden Rule, "treat others the way we ourselves want to be treated," is the idea that in order to receive something, we get to be willing to give it too. So, if we want others to hear our truth, we must be willing to hear theirs.

Remember that hearing another person's truth doesn't necessarily mean owning that truth or taking it on as yours. It means listening, holding the space for that person to communicate, and being open to them being open in your presence.

***

Speaking of presence, the third agreement is to *be present*.

Most of our worries don't come from things that exist in the present moment, rather they come from things we remember in the past or things we anticipate will happen in the future.

Whatever the situation, presence for me is about letting go of my attachment to specific outcomes. It means focusing on the other person while they're talking, instead of thinking about or planning what I'm going to say, why I'm going to say it, and what I hope will happen by saying it. I focus on *their words*, while at the same time keeping an eye on the rear view mirror of my mind, so to speak, noticing the sensations that arise in my body in response to those words. Perhaps even more important, I can start to hear what is *not* being said, which is sometimes evident by the speaker's mannerisms, inflection, posture, and facial expression. If I do get distracted by my own thoughts, to the degree that I feel that I'm not hearing the other person accurately, I might say, "Hey wait a second: I got lost there and want to catch up." It's less of an interruption than one might think, and more often than not the person I'm talking to is grateful that I want to be sure I understand them. Sometimes, if the person repeats what they said in order to catch me up, they realize the thing that they originally said was not the thing they meant to say, or that it meant something different.

A good rule of thumb: Listen to another person as if you had to teach someone else what they said immediately after.

If this idea makes conversations seem endless, I might be tempted to ask what's the hurry? We're at a retreat, and maybe the other stuff can wait, because it will still be there when you go home. I can't guarantee it will be there, and that's the point—to experiment with the notion that everything can wait, and if it can't or won't, to be ok it.

***

The fourth agreement is to *refrain from violence and threatening language.*

As you may expect, sometimes emotions come up in these retreats that might not have been dealt with for a while, and when they do it sometimes feels like a volcano or a geyser or a dam breaking. It's important for everyone to remember in those moments that these are signs of the emotional processing that's taking place, and to allow that process to flow without deflecting it or throwing it off onto someone else with violence or threatening language. Where violence begins, connection ends. This includes, obviously, physical aggression and unwanted contact, but also spitting and unwanted sexual attention, using threats, and speaking over others. Furthermore, these are all examples of being used by one's emotions rather than the other way around.

This agreement ensures that the space we are entering into is *co-created*, rather than hijacked or taken by force.

***

The fifth agreement is to *ask for what you want, and don't be attached to getting it.*

How many times do you want something and not say anything about it? Maybe it's a French fry, or a beverage, or it's something you want to do, a place you want to go, an idea you'd like other people to consider, or a question you want to ask. Whatever the desire, this is a space to practice the art of honoring yourself—your heart, your soul—enough to raise your hand and ask for it. Or don't raise your hand, depending on the context. (Maybe you're asking someone between activities if they'd like to go for a walk with you, in which case I probably wouldn't raise my hand. But then again…)

The reason for this agreement is because not asking for something we desire, whether it's out of shyness or shame or fear of the reaction, is a great way to not honor ourselves, and to shut ourselves down. Which may lead to resentment, towards one's self and others. Also, think of the burden that is unwittingly placed on whoever might be around us. It's like we expect them to pick up on what we want through ESP, and then blaming them in secret when they don't.

Asking for what one wants is an extension of telling the truth. Not being attached to getting it, on the other hand, is about acknowledging that other people are not in this world to do as we please simply because we please. They are in this world to do as they please, according to their truth and their desires. Personally, I wouldn't want another person to give me something simply because they were obliged to, or because they felt like they should, or because they were trying to manipulate me into giving something back. I would much rather they give me what they want to give me simply because they want to give it.

A note here about giving: my friend and author Brandon Hawk says when we give beyond our capacity, we make the receiver a thief. By the same token, when others give to us beyond their capacity, they might start to view us as thieves.

***

The sixth agreement is to *let go of saying you're sorry*.

I think there's a tendency in some parts of our culture to be overly apologetic, to say we're sorry so often that it's almost like a conditioned response. Two people reach the water fountain at the same time—one or both apologizes. A woman comes out of the bathroom after relieving herself and sees someone else waiting to enter—she apologizes and slinks away. Someone stretches out and accidentally bumps someone sitting nearby—"Sorry." What are they really sorry for? An outside observer, after hearing people say it so many times for so many things, might logically conclude that those people were sorry for everything, even their own existence. To take it even further, perhaps into conspiracy theory, I sometimes wonder if people are conditioned to say they're sorry because those in power know that language is powerful and that "the Word becomes Flesh." The more they can get other people to say they're sorry, the sorrier those people may become, and the easier they are to control.

Like all the other agreements, this one isn't permanent and binding for all time. This is a temporary agreement: for a time, we're going to play around with not saying we're sorry. Or, if and when we catch ourselves saying sorry or on the verge of saying sorry, we agree to explore that feeling out loud with the other person.

(Side note about pooping: Seriously, humans have got to be the only animal in the world that apologizes for pooping—a normal function of a healthy body that literally, and perhaps metaphorically, keeps it from being full of it. The word "sorry," in my opinion, can keep some people spiritually, emotionally, and psychologically constipated. To me it's every bit related to physical constipation, and might be one of the biggest health challenges people have faced.)

***

The seventh agreement is to *stay with conversations until those involved have reached a state of completion.*

Again, things are going to come up over the course of this retreat, and when they do we're going to talk about them, and that talk might catalyze other things coming up, and other participants joining, and that's why we agree to stick with those conversations beforehand, to keep us encouraged to have them.

One of the worst ways to have a conversation is not to have it, or to be on the verge of something and have it cut abruptly short by someone else. This agreement is about letting go of the four "normal" stress responses—flight, fight, freeze, and façade—which I believe are also the four biggest ways people used to sabotage themselves, and stepping into a new response, which I like to call *funcomfortable*.

This agreement, coupled with the idea of not giving beyond my own capacity, has inspired me a few times on retreats to say, "Hey, if anyone has something to bring up to me, I am ok with that until 10pm. After that, even if I stay up and don't go to bed, it might not be within my capacity to stick with a conversation to the end. So, in that case, I would ask that you wait until tomorrow to bring it up."

***

The eighth and final agreement is to *expect nothing, and experience everything*.

Or you could upgrade that to expect anything, experience everything, but the goal here is to experience. Not to go into situations wanting them to turn out a certain way, being so attached to that imagined outcome that we lose touch with what is actually happening. We're all going into this retreat, this experience, as students. We agree, therefore, to be open to the experience unfolding. It means not to go with the flow, but to *glow and grow with the flow*. Let go and let God.

Quantum growth takes place within your funcomfort zone.

Chapter 3

Polar Plunge

Typically, the first thing we do is get in the water.

Preferably *cold* water, either right there at the retreat location or a short drive away. We've plunged in rivers, in lakes, in ponds; we've jumped off bridges and cliffs into the ocean below, swam into hidden tidal lagoons, and showered beneath waterfalls. You name it. If the water is cold and clean and reasonably safe, we get in.

The reason is water, that vital element which covers most of our planet and supports all the life it contains. Water, which is not the element we live in, but the one we are made of and depend upon. Water, which is formless, shapeless, and fills any container. Water, which is soft, as Bruce Lee noted, but powerful enough to crush rocks.

I imagine that early baptisms, before there were churches and tap water and the strict observance of rituals, probably took place out in nature, outside the city or settlement, either in forests or plains or along the coast. People would have traveled to get there, some from long distances, perhaps days away, so that the journey itself became a part of the process. By the time they got to the "holy" site, whether a river or ocean or falls, they were primed to receive the spirit, not by thinking about it or around it, but by immersing themselves in it.

The Self we are speaks to us not only through our thoughts but also through our bodies, in the form of physical sensations. I believe in the recent past, when those sensations got too strong, beyond what we wanted or thought we were capable of handling, there was a cultural push towards numbing sensations with drugs or painkillers, depressants and anti-depressants, or trying to make them go away altogether by thinking about something else. In this day and age, where there's a drug for just about every symptom, and where the amount of control we can exercise over our environment is greater than it's ever been before, what with things like architecture and science and heating and air-conditioning, it's almost like there's a taboo against feeling any way other than normal or neutral. Not too hot, not too cold. It's astounding the number of things we have at our disposal to keep us in a state of perpetual comfort: ice cubes, microwaves, Jacuzzi jets, electric blankets, robes, slippers, wetsuits, fans, dehumidifiers, recliners, not to mention alcohol and coffee and sugar and cannabis and cold medicine and cough drops and alkalizers and decongestants. Not that I'm against any of those, or against any of the other modern blessings we have, but I'm also not against feeling whatever it is those things were invented to cover up: hot, cold, sad, mad, hungry, bloated, tired, energized, sorrow, pain, etc. In fact, in many cases, I've found that it was my resistance to feeling those feelings, rather than the feelings themselves, that was the true source of my discomfort and suffering. When I allowed them to happen—when I allowed myself to feel them—the feeling got better.

Why would anyone not want to feel things, when feeling is one of the ways we know we're alive? That's why we have bodies. If we didn't have them, how would we know how we felt, or where we were, or what we're doing, or where we're headed?

That's why we jump in: to get out of our heads and into our bodies. Because over time what can happen amidst all our comfort is that we forget how to feel, not only all the so-called bad things that we didn't want to feel in the first place, but the good things too. Everything gets suppressed or mediated through the head. It reminds me of the perspectives, "Man invented the wheel and forgot how to walk" and "The path you find yourself on can become the path you lose yourself on."

We prefer to jump in cold water because it's pretty much guaranteed to make you feel something. As soon as I hit the water, it's such an instant rush of sensation that whatever I was thinking about or worrying about or distracted by is immediately pushed to the side. There is nothing but the water which is cold, and my body which is alive.

It turns out that getting cold, something we might have balked at in the past, is actually good for us in certain doses. It seems like every day, either on YouTube or Facebook or some other media outlet, there is something about the benefits of cold. This has contributed to the growing popularity of cryotherapy, polar plunging, and Wim Hof. Benefits include reduced inflammation, blood circulation, pumping the lymphatic system, and burning fat. Personally, whenever I've had a headache, brain fog, or felt tired in general, a polar plunge has worked better than coffee or pills. And I love coffee.

That alone is reason enough to get in the water, but the main reason we do it is to wake up the sensations we may have been suppressing.

***

Not surprisingly, not everyone wants to get in. "That's crazy," they think. "It'll make me sick." Or they're already cold and don't want to do anything to make it worse. Or they don't have swimsuits. Or they just washed their hair. Or any number of other limiting stories.

There was a woman at one of our winter retreats (I'll call her *Meredith*) who, when she arrived, noticed that she was older than the other attendees, and I imagine that catalyzed a story in her head went something like this: "I signed up for this retreat feeling super excited, but now that I'm here I see it's mostly twenty-something year-olds and I feel out of place. *I'm forty.* Probably the only one here who's married with kids." Something of the sort seemed to be going on with her initially, but nowhere was it more obvious than when we drove out to Deer Lake with the intention of getting in the water. Mind you, it was wintertime, and cold, and the sky was overcast. When we pulled up, the water was perfectly still, with snow-covered mountains visible in the distance. Our retreat had just gotten started and most people were riding a wave of excitement, generally talkative and making playful, ominous references to the water. Our breath was visible in the air. This was not exactly the time of the year one normally associates with swimming outdoors. As we put on our swimsuits, Meredith noticed that her own energy seemed lower than everyone else's. She explained to us later that she seemed to be the only one not amped up. The water to her wasn't inviting so much as intimidating. Nonetheless, she got into her swimsuit and waded out with the rest of the group, until the water came up to her waist. The water was cold, and some people whooped and cheered while others sucked air in loudly through their lips. Meredith got quiet, and stayed mostly to herself. Not wanting to stand out in a negative way, she pretended to be enjoying it, made small talk with some of the others who didn't go out past waist-level, while secretly counting down for the exercise to be over. When someone else was the first one out of the water, she immediately followed, without having dunked her head.

Perhaps that's what Meredith had in mind for the retreat in general: a dipping of the toes rather than a full-body immersion. Whatever feeling had compelled her a few months prior to go out on a limb and reach out to someone she'd seen on Facebook (me), that feeling was gone, replaced by the desire not to experience the experience, but to survive and get through.

When it was time to go, we all dried off and got dressed and hopped back into the cars. Meredith, who had offered her minivan as one of the retreat vehicles, got behind the wheel, put the car in drive, inched forward a little, and then stopped.

It was a moment of decision, and she looked out the window in silence.

She became consciously aware of the story she was telling herself, the one that said because she was "older" and a mother she would not fully participate in the activities, but rather "keep an eye out while the kids played."The awareness was a clue: If she were at home right now, what would she be doing? Probably she'd be comfy and cozy on her own couch with her own family. But also, she realized, she'd probably be watching videos about people on retreats, the very ones she had been watching when she decided to take a leap of faith and come, videos of people jumping into cold water, and coming out looking rejuvenated and refreshed. In short, this moment is exactly what she wanted. She wanted to come out here and dive into the experience, literally and metaphorically, but then when she got to the retreat she allowed the story she was telling herself to get in the way.

With that she smacked the steering wheel and announced, "Guys, I'm getting in that water."

So that's what she did. She got out of the car, back into her swimsuit, the bottom piece still wet and cold from her previous dip, took her hoodie off and waded out once more. The rest of us stood on shore and watched quietly. Her inner child was showing through. When she was far enough out that the water came to her chest, she turned around, gave us a part-smile, part-grimace from the cold, and then went under, disappearing below the surface.

At that moment, she said later, a weight on her shoulders lifted, and the retreat began.

***

There is a well-known experiment in post-hypnotic suggestion, in which a subject is put under hypnosis and told that when he wakes up he will get up, go outside, open his umbrella, come back in and sit down. Sure enough, when the subject is brought out of it he gets up, goes outside, opens his umbrella, comes back in and sits down. "Why did you do that?" the psychologist asks. And the subject answers, "Because I'm going out with friends later and it might rain, so I wanted to make sure my umbrella was working."

Here's the thing: He's telling the truth so far as he consciously "knows" it. If you hooked him up to a lie detector test, he'd probably pass. The experiment is worth noting here because the results of it suggest that it's possible to be under the direct control of someone or something else and not know it. So, the question is, how do we know we're not hypnotized? If not directly by a psychologist, perhaps indirectly—by routine, a group of people, our own thoughts.

On a cultural and societal level, hypnosis works as follows: a population is overfed, undernourished, sleep-deprived, cut off from nature, and dependent on drugs they can only get from those in power. They are surrounded by modern convenience and material things, kept "comfortable" and "stimulated" and distracted by the "news" piped directly into their homes—bigger elections, threats of violence, fears of scarcity. A society that is scared is easy to manipulate and open to subconscious messaging, because they allowed themselves to lose touch with their innate wisdom and discernment. They behave in false ways and make up reasons for it after the fact, reasons they perpetuate and spread to other people. Reasons that may sound normal—"I wanted to make sure my umbrella was working"—but which from a different perspective don't reflect the whole truth. Their opinions, then, are not truly theirs, and they argue for limitations they've been conditioned to have.

***

The psychologist might snap or clap or drop the subject to wake him up, but the way we do it is to jump in cold water.

Initially it can be jarring, maybe unpleasant. It's like the human equivalent of going from zero to sixty in an instant: physically, everything to turns on. The first thing some people think is holy heavens, I want to get out. And if they do, that's great. At least they got in, got cold. Not mentally cold, not imaginatively cold, and not cold because someone told them they were cold, but really and truly cold. So cold that it might feel hot, almost burning— same thing. They're having a direct experience and getting direct feedback.

With practice and conditioning, you can learn to observe and not give into that first reaction to get out of the water. You can grow to accept the sensation, acknowledge it, breathe into it, and let it pass. Your heartbeat slows, your chattering jaws calm down, your limbs remain under control. You realize that not only are you ok, you're better than ok, stronger and more capable than you know.

***

That's why we get in the water at the beginning, as a show of agreement that for the next few days, we are willing to go outside of our comfort zones and play in more watery environments, emotionally speaking, exploring their depths and surprises. We do it to say yes. Yes to the experience, yes to ourselves, yes to life. Because the moment of letting go and jumping in, that's what it feels like.

What you're running away from is chasing you, and what you're attached to getting is running away from you.

Chapter 4

Feeling Is Healing

They say water is the source of life on Earth, and that the best, healthiest water is artesian spring water. No, that's not "artisanal," as in ultra-spiritual artsy-fartsy water. It's simply water that comes from a place in the ground, a well, where natural pressure deep in the Earth forces the water up to the surface.

How deep? Very deep. In some cases, miles deep. That makes the water that comes out old, perhaps ten thousand years old. It's water that originally fell as rain or snow a long time ago, and ever so slowly seeped into the Earth, far down to where the heat and pressure eventually forced it back up to the surface. In the process, it was mineralized. Sometimes, it even tastes sulfuric. It is clean water, untouched by surface contamination.

Compare that to the water it seems like many people in the industrialized world drink, either bottled up or from the tap: purified, demineralized, chemically cleaned, injected with fluoride, and sometimes laced with trace amounts of drugs and antidepressants from the collective's urine, contaminated by pesticide runoff, and even laden with heavy metals. Fluoride, furthermore, originally added to drinking water for "dental purposes," has been shown to have unintended side effects. One of those side effects is calcification of the pineal gland, which in some eastern and more "primitive" health systems represents the third eye, our connection to divine intelligence. Some say that fluoride acts as a neurotoxin, which is why it is added to the public water supply—to keep the populace docile. That's the water that is still deemed by many authorities to be safe, and for that reason many people drink it. Safe, meaning harmless, unlikely to upset the system.

***

Each of us, emotionally, is our own spring. It seems like all the time there are things bubbling up within me, and even when it might feel like there's nothing, there's still something.

What that something is is not so much a physical thing as an energetic thing, and for that matter, a wave. That's what emotion is, energy in motion. We've all seen and felt the effects of too much energy in motion, usually after it's been pent up or repressed, in the form of volcanoes or outbursts or breaking dams. We've also seen and felt the effects of too much energy not in motion, in the form of stagnation and pollution and depression. The energy affects our bodies, depending on its flow. It affects our muscles, our breathing, our perspiration, but also, deeper down, it affects our hormones, our organ and bowel function, and probably (more like certainly) it affects the chemical and electrical processes in our brains.

Emotions produce sensations, but unlike sensations that come from outside, these come from inside. They may seem deep, mysterious, dangerous, or casual, superficial, passing. Maybe some of them do come from thousands of years ago, passed down through familial, racial, national, or tribal memory. Regardless, it's all energy, and the more aware we can be of our own energy, the more we can allow it to flow to the surface, where metaphorically, it can be nourishing and vital to us.

***

In light of all this, there are a few exercises we do on retreats to get in touch with the sensations in our bodies, and more specifically, the ones that are normally harder and more intimidating to handle, especially those that arise in the presence of another person.

The first exercise is *Eye-Gazing*. We partner up facing one another, not so close that our noses are touching, but pretty close, slightly too close for comfort, and then we gaze into each other's eyes.

This is such a simple exercise, but one that brings up so many emotions and feelings. And it only takes a few minutes. The only rule, or guideline, is to look into the other person's eyes as long as you can, and if you blink or look away, to gently come back into focus. Do your best not to talk, gesture, move around, or try to express anything in any obvious way. Don't force a straight face, but don't force a scowl or smile either. Keep looking. Maintain eye contact past the sticking point where you feel tempted to look away.

It's surprising how much can come up simply by looking at someone and having them look at you. I notice all sorts of sensations right away, dozens of tiny waves throughout my body, or a surge of thoughts up in my head. Some parts of me may feel tingly, warmer, colder, or different from the rest. The urge to communicate is strong, sometimes almost unbearable, and even though you may try to suppress it, try to hold it in (there's that word I "try" not to use).

The exercise can break out of you in all sorts of   ways, from laughter to repetitive physical tics to staring to swaying. Keep your focus, first on the sensation, then on yourself experiencing the sensation, and then concentrate on making that sensation more of what it is. See if it can be amplified, breathing with it as you do, feeling your way deeper into it, getting grounded emotionally.

Of course, at the same time all this is happening there's the other person's face right there in front of you, a face that in my experience suddenly presents itself, in all its many details, in a miraculous light. And the wearer of that face, the person behind it and through it— a singular phenomenon. It's as if he or she takes on another dimension, like I'm seeing them more clearly, getting a glimpse of their Y-O-Universe.

To be sure, you might notice different sensations with different people, and those sensations might be associated in your mind with different stories. With some you might squirm uncomfortably, with others you'll be more at ease. You might notice sensations come up that you normally associate with feeling competitive or aggressive, in which case perhaps you start staring at that other person in order to blink and look away. Towards others you might convey graciousness and acceptance with your eyes, emoting good things to them.

Whatever it is, as soon as you notice it, you can gently come back into focus, and sit with the feeling of your energy as distinct from theirs. It's really a balancing act, in a way, this dual-attention within and without. The thing to realize is that in this space we've co-created it's ok, more than ok, to fall. Maybe it's through falling that one learns to harness the fear of falling. Over time I have noticed a softening effect, a growing acceptance of myself in another's presence, and their self in mine. It's a matter of intention, I believe—to *be* rather than act or react, to use heart and head.

***

Sometimes we do this exercise with a partner, for a target time of, say, two minutes, and sometimes we do it as a group, in which case it proceeds more organically. We sit or stand in a close circle, and begin by locking eyes with the first person we happen to turn towards. The same guidelines as before still apply, and the goal is to maintain eye-contact past that sticking point. Only this time, instead of a timer signaling when to stop, we break eye-contact with the person in front of us when it feels natural and mutual to do so, whereupon we turn to towards the next person, and do it again.

Afterward, when the time is up, we talk to our partners and amongst ourselves about what happened, what we experienced.

There's a variation we like to throw in as well: Rather than having both people remain silent while staring, we take turns having one of them speak non-stop. Really, non-stop, regardless of how silly or stupid the speaker may think they sound, to the point of babbling or counting numbers if need be. The goal is to keep going through it, allowing oneself to be silly and spontaneous. The goal for the other person, meanwhile, is to remain as stoic as possible, to stay rooted in their own sensations as they listen.

For the person speaking, this variation forces him or her to say whatever it is he or she wants to say (or whatever it is that comes up) without the encouragement of the subtle social cues most listeners will often provide in conversation. This includes bobble-heading, expressions of acknowledgment with the eyes, saying "uh-huh" or "uh-uh" or "yes" or "no." These are all the habits and tics, largely unconscious, we may use to provide reassurance to the person we are listening to. For the person listening, this variation catalyzes two things: being aware of one's energy in response to what the other person is saying; and through sitting with it, becoming more energetically self-sufficient.

***

The second exercise we do is called *Notice and Imagine.* The purpose of this exercise is to disentangle, and gain clarity between, what we feel and what we think, between our sensations, on the one hand, and the things we think about them, on the other.

Similar to the previous exercise, you begin by standing face to face with a partner, close but not too close. Then, one at a time, you take turns saying something you notice, followed by something you imagine from it. For example: "I notice your eyebrows, and I imagine a caterpillar."

At first, a lot of people try to be smarter than the exercise. They try to sound clever or profound or deep. Simply looking at someone and saying, "I notice your eyes, I notice your hair, I notice my body shaking" sounds too simple, or so they think. Instead I hear things like, "I notice you're judging my face." "I notice that you're angry or upset." "I notice you feel nervous." That's when I step in and ask, "What exactly do you notice about that person's expression that catalyzes you to imagine they're judging your face? What do you notice that makes you imagine he or she is angry? What sensations in your body do you associate with being nervous?" I then tell the participants to turn their brains off and allow themselves to be in a state that they might ordinarily consider extremely elementary or simple. "Like a dog?" Exactly. Let's imagine, for example, that a dog's inner monologue goes something like this: "Eyes, eyes, eyes, nose, ball, squirrel..."

In the exercise, we do something similar: "I notice your eyes, I notice your mouth. I notice my palms sweating." It's a little more sophisticated than the dog's, but not much, and the reason for that level of simplicity, that level of obviousness, is to get in touch with reality, and distinguish it from all the stories and interpretations that go through our heads. In the first example ("I notice you're judging my face...") participants are not reporting what they notice; they are reporting stories about what they notice, rational lies about what they feel, without keeping the verbal distinction. Another person could observe the exact same face and imagine something completely different. He or she might observe a scowl, for example, or that the eyes seem narrow and focused, and from that observation imagine that the person was trying not to laugh. The point is that these stories sneak in so easily because the mind is good at making them. The challenge was that we didn't realize they were stories, and mistook them for reality. It might be the case that living a more "awakened" life involves not believing everything you think.

The language is a giveaway. Have you ever said or heard someone say, "I feel like..." followed by something that is not objective, not even close to a feeling? "I feel like you're judging me. I feel like so and so is making fun of someone else. I feel like..." Stop right there. Whatever is about to be said is highly subjective, a story, imaginary, and not something that another person, perhaps not even a dog or child, would necessarily recognize as true.

For example: "I feel angry." If someone says that to me I'm not sure how exactly they feel. But if they say, "I feel tense, wound up, and my face is hot," I have a better idea of how they feel. Queasy stomach, tight shoulders, dizziness, fatigue, shaking—those sound more like feelings to me, and none of them automatically translates to the names we are prone to attach to them, like anger, fear, or excitement. Many people feel suspiciously similar sensations, like flushed cheeks, but when I ask how they feel, they say opposite things: one says excited while the other says scared. What one person calls anger another person might call confusion. What one person calls confusion another might call learning. It's not that strange an idea: the same feeling can produce two drastically different reactions. One person, reacting to sensations that we normally associate with fear, might lash out at someone else; another person, reacting to the same sensations, might go out and run five miles. It's not only possible, but it sometimes happens, that you laugh until you cry, and you cry until you laugh. Sometimes you cry when you're happy, and laugh when you're sad. The point is that it's hard to tell, by looking alone, exactly how someone is feeling. Similarly, regarding your own feelings, it is wise to notice them and feel them and not jump to conclusions. Those conclusions are stories. By sharing them and acknowledging them as stories, one gains separation from them. It's also a *funcomfortable* form of self-acceptance through self-expression.

Before long, with a little practice, the conversations begin to sound like this:

"I notice your eyes pointing at my cheek, and I imagine it's because I have something on my face."

"I notice my legs feel shaky, and I imagine it's because I'm nervous. And I imagine I'm nervous because a part of me wants to make a good impression on you."

"I notice you standing in a way that I imagine I would stand if I was experiencing anger."

"I notice your teeth and I imagine they are extremely white and well formed, and I imagine it's because your parents were healthy when they had you."

"I notice your shoulders, and I imagine they are slumped over, and that your posture might be better if your muscles were less tight."

That's the way someone talks who understands the difference between reality and delusion. Those sentences above come from people who are aware of the stories in their heads, and on guard against heartlessly projecting them onto the world around them.

***

There's a story I've heard about a woman in an asylum who seemed perfectly normal. She was serene, soft-spoken, and according to everyone who knew her—before the asylum and during—she was altogether pleasant to be around. She'd always been that way. She was locked up, though, because as it turned out, the serenity was only a façade. In truth, she was so tightly wound from constantly trying to keep her emotions under wrap that one day she snapped. She murdered her aunt, cut her into pieces, put her in a bathtub, and afterward went back to normal. The police who apprehended her could not imagine that a woman so pleasant was capable of such violence.

Here's the thing about both water and emotions: they cannot be stopped indefinitely. You can dam them, funnel them, channel them, et cetera, but eventually they're coming out. Where there is damming, there is damning, condemned emotions held back. This is how the ocean of our emotion, which is deep and magnificent, becomes scary, intimidating, or even stagnant and polluted. Rather than celebrate it for the dynamic, inexhaustible well it is, we turn it into a hiding place for our so-called nasty parts.

The bigger the dam the more water it holds back, the more pressure it is under.

**

It's the same with our emotions. The example of the woman is not that unique. Why is it that whenever we see someone on TV who's been arrested after carrying out a violent rampage, that person often seems dazed and confused, almost as if they're drugged? It's because (I imagine) they've blacked out and released a ton of pent up energy and emotion, resulting in a feeling of detachment and emptiness they aren't used to. They've discharged so much aggression, so much anger, so much pain and fear and maybe even happiness and love—all of it repressed and withheld—that they are now devoid of feeling. That might be why you rarely see them lash out in court. Instead, they seem almost catatonic. When pressed by investigators and prosecutors as to why they did such a thing, they seem eerily detached and clinical. They aren't sure why they did it, so, like the umbrella man under hypnosis, they reach for some kind of story. The unfortunate part is, I imagine a lot of them realize too late and after the fact that they didn't need to do what they did, that the course of action they chose was destructive and unnecessary.

The goal emotionally is to let the water flow, to feel what you're feeling in the moment you actually feel it. Holding it in raises the likelihood that it will come out later. Isn't that the nature of so-called destructive emotions, not the emotion itself, but that we release it at a deflective time, or in misguided, exaggerated way, or at the wrong person altogether? Imagine a pebble dropping into water but not producing any ripples because the water held them in. It would look strange and not quite natural. Imagine a surfer trying to ride a wave that's already passed. It would not only be futile, but also dangerous. Her back would be turned to the oncoming waves, which could toss her back and forth or knock her off the board.

I don't know about you, but I've noticed in my own life that it feels a lot healthier and natural to let my emotions flow in the moment rather than alternately dam and erupt. "Healthier" and "natural," however, aren't really feelings, so let me be more specific: I notice that my body feels looser, more mobile, less depressed (in the sense of a low energy) and more vitalized than it did when I was not sharing or expressing my emotions. Maybe a yogi would describe this as all chakras being open and in flow. It feels good, which again is vague, so I'll specify: I feel energized, aligned, peaceful, capable.

When you fully feel an experience, it comes and goes. When you resist it, however, it tends to persist. Maybe the resistance starts unconsciously, and then manifests itself as sensations in the body. In that case, I'd say when you notice those sensations of resistance, don't resist them. Instead observe, question, and experiment. See what you can do to help the sensations flow. Share them out loud.

"I notice my chest is tight and my jaw is shaking. I imagine it might be a sign that I'm feeling triggered or in the past I might have said angry. But maybe I'm just cold.

"I notice sensations of fatigue or heaviness in my body, and I imagine that I don't really want to do anything right now, or that I'm having a dip in energy or even depression."

"I notice a lot of sensations in my body when I think about this particular person, and I imagine it's because I want to talk to them about something I consider to be important."

Noticing and imagining is not always a black and white situation; it can be a very gray area. It is helpful though, even in the gray zones, to err on the side of the extreme and really distinguish between the sensation you are having (noticing), and the interpretation you have of that sensation (imagining). This kind of process, the care we take with language, is not only a matter of speaking more clearly, it's a matter of thinking more clearly. Reality is not the delusion we carry in our heads. It's this strange thing outside of us, which we can observe and modify, but which is also changing and a fun challenge to grasp. When you move, it moves too. When you attack from head on, it ducks and maneuvers. An upgraded strategy might be to sneak up on it, in a way, to approach it from behind. This kind of thinking allows you to do that, to sneak up on the truth indirectly, before it runs away. Emotionally, it's like catching ourselves in the act, observing the wave or ripple of emotion coming up in us before it arrives. This method is not passive or repressive or blindly reactive. It's not new-age or touch-feely. It might be one of the most important keys to health and high performance. It's the difference between being angry, on the one hand, and noticing sensations that you normally associate with anger, on the other. In the former you become your anger, while in the latter you evolve through the emotion—using it, rather than being used.

Elliott Hulse, in his book *King*, raises the idea that when someone thinks more than they move, they get trapped in their own heads, which is fertile ground for insanity. Similarly, when people think about their emotions (or around them) rather than expressing them in a healthy way, they might be creating more challenges for themselves down the road.

Feelings are like the "check engine" lights of our individual vehicles. They come on in order to get our attention, to signal something to us, something that is beneficial to be done, perhaps, or something coming up on the horizon.

You don't get mad, I imagine, when the low-fuel light comes on when in fact your car is low on gas. On the contrary, I imagine that you probably thank it in your head and affirm it for looking out for you, for keeping track of something so that you can focus on other things. You relax. You don't have to worry about everything. You don't have to hold in your mind the tire pressure, the oil level, the transmission fluid, the engine heat, and all the other things all at once. The car looks out for you in the same way that you look out for it. It keeps its mind on certain details so you can keep yours on others.

In the same way, your deeper self, like your car, naturally looks out for you too. This Self, which I believe is closely connected with the Creator, is looking out for your life and sending you clues and signals along the way. One of the ways it sends signals to you is through your feelings, the sensations that come on in your body.

One of these signals, for example, is boredom. Ideally you would catch this feeling in the form of physical sensations (or lack thereof) before it gets interpreted and charged by your mind as something like boredom, because think about it, it really does show up in your body first.

Does it sometimes happen that, when you're in conversation with someone else, you suddenly notice that something in your body doesn't quite feel right? The way you're standing feels uncomfortable, for example, or awkward; the way you're holding your hands seems unnatural; even the expression on your face seems not exactly in sync. All these little lights go off in you, and the more you notice them, the more your energy sort of rises and concentrates in your head. Boredom is that gradually increasing awareness that your mind is distracted, that you aren't wholly invested or interested in whatever you're currently doing. Literally, your mind is elsewhere, flashing forward into the future or backward into the past, which can make your head feel off or incongruent.

I've found that when this engine light comes on it's a signal for me to get back in my body by letting the steam out, by calling out the feelings I notice, and expressing and expelling the stories my mind comes up with about them. It's amazing, one of the fastest ways to get un-bored is to call out your boredom, to say to the other person, "I sort of zoned out when you were talking. I noticed sensations in my body that I imagine signal boredom, like I'm not fully present with this moment." It's amazing how fast that can change the conversation, because sometimes, the other person feels it too but didn't want to say anything.

What happens in your car when you ignore the "50 Miles to Empty" alert? It dings again at 25. Ignore that one and it will go off again at 15, then at 10, at 5. In some cars, the signal might even get louder and more insistent the longer you ignore it without taking action or changing course. If you ignore the signals you might end up stranded on the side of the road.

What happens when you ignore the "Fasten Seat Belt" reminder? It beeps again and again and again. Eventually it blares non-stop.

What you resist tends to persist, and continues to persist as long as you resist it. As soon as you say it, which means first noticing that you're feeling it, you stop resisting it, and the engine light turns off.

You get what you give, and you
see what you are looking for.

Chapter 5

Self-Acceptance through Self-Expression

At a recent playshop an older man shared a dream he'd previously had. He was climbing a mountain, getting closer to the top, but also feeling tired and weighed down. He was wearing a backpack, which at first seemed normal, until he realized that he had no idea what was in it, no idea why he had packed it, and no reason to continue carrying it up the mountain. To reach the top, he decided, he would have to drop it.

He mentioned this dream in the context of the next exercise, *Confession*. The backpack, he decided, was full of stories that were no longer useful to him, that held him back in his growth as a person. They were stories about what he could and couldn't do, based on the "fact" that he was such and such type of person. They were memories of memories of incidences from his past, things that he still carried shame about, things that happened years ago which, when he thought about them, still had the power to make him feel embarrassed. He realized that he had packed this backpack, not all at once, but over the course of his life. Every time he stopped himself from fully feeling an experience, the backpack got heavier. Every time he allowed emotions like fear to prevent him from doing something that a *funcomfortable* voice inside him wanted to do, the backpack got heavier. Every time he rationalized about why it had to be so, when deeper down he knew better, the backpack got heavier.

How do you get rid of the backpack? You get honest. It sounds easy, it sounds cliché. Clichés are popular, however, because a lot of people recognize their inherent truth. Like most clichés, there's a lot more to them than initially meets the eye.

The first step to getting honest is to start talking about the ways in which we might have lied in the past. Emerson says, "Commit a crime, and the world is made of glass." Lying is exactly that sort of crime. It turns the ground to glass that we fear we'll break with every step. So, we start to tiptoe, and when we tiptoe, we're tense. Tension causes stress and stress can cause dis-ease. By restricting our breathing, creating energetic blockages, and damming emotions, stress leads to fatigue, hormonal imbalance, and even changes in our internal pH. Disease thrives in tense, acidic environments.

The most insidious, most prevalent form of lying is withholding, which is not saying something we want to say because we fear the reaction. The thing one withholds doesn't go away. It stays within like a land mine. The more people withhold, the more land mines they gather. After a while they can't even play or relax anymore, because there are so many mines in the yard, so to speak, that they might step on one at any moment. Others can't play or relax around them, because it's dangerous—one wrong word and they might blow up (that is, blow up on them). The land mines surround them and bisect them. They cut people off from themselves and cut them off from other people.

Lying fills them up with waste, leads to heaviness and constipation. Whether it's withholding, partial withholding, telling white lies or speaking slander altogether, the end result is that they don't get it out. When they lie about something they create a gap between the person they're pretending to be and the person they really are. It takes a lot of energy to maintain that gap, and the more energy that goes into maintaining it the less energy there is to put into the things that might matter more, like their goals and pursuits. In that way, lying is a form of self-sabotage. Their light gets dim because of all the stories they layer on top of it. Similar to covering their body in shame and shutting their emotions down in fear, they start putting filters on what they say. They think before they speak, and neurotically daily bite their tongue.

That's the road that leads out of the garden, paved though it might be with "good" intentions. The lies this road is made of are sometimes big but they are more often small white lies. Taken one at a time, they seem inconsequential, benign. The lies are casual, and in some cases even expected. Passing someone on the street, for example, and asking them how they are, a lot of people don't expect an honest answer, and when they themselves are asked, they rarely give one. "I'm fine," they say, and move along. They get in the habit of not sharing their authentic opinions or spontaneous impressions as they spring to mind. They try to hide them, along with their insecurities, fears, and judgments. When someone else is talking and they either don't agree or don't feel like listening, they nod their heads mechanically and politely so as not to be rude, meanwhile deceiving that other person by implying that they understand and agree. "Oh well," they might rationalize (which means rationally lie), "the more I nod my head the sooner they'll stop talking…it's not worth the trouble of telling the truth."

As four-year-olds we probably wouldn't do that. If someone asked us back then, for example, whether we liked their outfit, we would have given a quick and honest answer. We would have faithfully reported what came up in us in response to the question. Ask that same question a few years later, however, and by then a lot of people would probably have learned to hedge a bit, meaning they would first think it over and play the answer a few times in their minds, and then change it based on how they thought the questioner would react. Imagine the toll that takes when one does it every day. It seems like the older they got, the more frequently they had to do it, simply to survive, to get by, make friends, please their teachers, preachers, and relatives. Fast-forward twenty years or so and what do we have? An adult, a grown-up, which today can mean someone whose truth is so complicated, so guarded by land mines, that they don't express it, maybe don't even hear it because of all the noise.

That's the situation a lot of people are in. That's the challenge to overcome. They're emotionally constipated, full of other people's stories and "why, because" rationalizations that keep them trapped in the jail of their minds. They talk differently in public than they do in private, and there is a gap between what they say and how they act. Whenever that gap is exposed they feel vulnerable and cover it up as quickly as possible. They might have thought that lying, withholding, and biting their tongue was basic social intelligence, a way to get by and not make waves. They might have thought that riding the tide of least resistance would land them on the island of success. Instead they are marooned, surrounded by land mines, prison bars, out of touch with what they actually think and feel.

They withheld their gifts and their strengths, their weaknesses and doubts. They lied about the things they didn't want other people to know about them, out of fear of rejection, and they lied about the things they did want people to know about them, also, paradoxically, out of fear of rejection. That fear of rejection is often a cover for the fear of intimacy. They made themselves out to be both better and worse than they were. It was false virtue and false modesty, a desire to please others to such an extent that they stopped listening to and honoring themselves.

The key to freedom is at the tip of their nose, but like Pinocchio every time they lie or bite their tongue that nose grows a little bit bigger. The guard of this jail is the mind that filters every thought. The way out of jail is to surprise the guard, to speak before they think, not after. If they wait to say the words coming up until after they've already thought about them, that is, until they are absolutely sure that the words are safe to say (safe, meaning innocuous, inoffensive, filtered, fluoridated) they will probably not say them at all. They will rationalize that the thing they were going to say was stupid or out of left field, that it would have offended the other person, that they didn't actually think it, that they didn't know if it was correct or something they made up. They will bite their tongue, and whatever it was that originally sparked those words within, possibly their heart and soul, will get the message that they aren't listening to it, and eventually, it will go quiet altogether.

***

The exercise we do is *Confession*. I love to think of it as social bungee-jumping. It's an invitation to unconditional love, and to let go of the addiction to fitting in. We get back in the circle and take turns saying all the things we don't want to say, telling the group all the things we don't want them to know about us.

Each person has two minutes, two minutes to black out and say whatever comes up that causes their palms to sweat, their hands to shake, and their hearts to beat the fastest. The riskier it sounds in your imagination, the more key it may be to your freedom.

The time limit is in place to keep the rationalizations and stories to a minimum. The goal of the exercise is to say these things somewhat quickly, before you can think your way around them. The role of the audience, in addition to staying present with each confession, is to listen for any hedging, any pulled punches, any rationalizations and stories. If they hear something that seems like an attempt to soften the blow, they can call out "Story" to get the confessor back on track.

I'm tempted here to explain the exercise further, but I'm even more tempted to show you what I mean by going first. I notice my heartbeat is elevated, and my mind is racing, and I imagine that means it's time. Besides, I love following my heart, especially when it seems *funcomfortable* to do so.

***

The first thing I don't want you to know is that when I was younger I had a reputation for being a reckless driver. I was once pulled over for doing 106 in a 70. My mom and sister were both sleeping in the car. I could have been arrested on the spot, but instead we followed the cop back to the station, whereupon my mom negotiated with him and got the ticket reduced to 99 in a 70.

When I was a junior in high school I flipped and totaled my mom's car, because I was trying to prove my physics teacher wrong about centripetal force as it pertained to the maximum speed a car could safely take the curve of our school's bus lane. My best friend was in the passenger seat videotaping. His hand was cut in the accident, but other than that, neither of us was hurt.

I once peed in a cup and told my brother it was orange juice. He didn't believe me, but he trusted me, his big brother, so when I told him to take a sip, he did.

Another time I asked to kiss him. I think I "just" wanted to practice on him so that when the time came to kiss a girl I'd know what to do, but who knows? I'm grateful that he refused me.

I ejaculated into my mouth once when I was a teenager. I'm not sure why. I didn't swallow, and I don't even remember now if I ejaculated directly into my mouth or if I just—

"Story."

I imagine you're judging me for that one, so I might as well share that I have a judgment about you: that you might be concealing some shadows of your own, shadows that you judge yourself for. To be totally honest, I've confessed that detail so many times that it's sort of lost its shock value. It doesn't even seem like a big deal anymore. I ejaculated into my mouth once—who cares?

"Story."

Let's see...I lost my virginity when I was twenty-two. The girl I lost it to knew it was my first time, and I think that made her happy in some way. Part of me believed premarital sex was a sin, according to the Bible. Another part of me just wanted to do it. My dad said it was ok as long as we used a condom. I listened to him because he is my parent and the Bible says to listen to your parents. When the moment came, I couldn't perform, so I chugged some alcohol to loosen up and help me last longer. Turns out, I lasted too long.

I once masturbated while thinking about another ex-girlfriend's mom. When I told her, she ended both our relationship and our friendship shortly thereafter.

Part of me worries that I'm not all that great at sex. I think I might be a lot better at a lot of other things. That's a reality I am currently upgrading though...Story.

Before I proposed to my now wife, I told her she wasn't "marriage material" referring to her religious views, which are different from mine and my family's, and my family takes issue with her for it. She and I have had fights about it.

What else? In the past year or so, I've smoked cannabis more days than not. I've drank more nights than not—two to a few beers before dinner. I used to smoke more sporadically, but lately, this past year or so, I'd say I smoked about ninety-five plus percent of the days, including when I was in states where using the herb is still illegal. I used to be shy about marijuana. I was afraid to admit that I liked it. But that was in the past. I love it. I recommend it for some people in the right context.

Sometimes I worried that hell is real, not metaphorical, and that I or my loved ones might end up there. On the other hand, I worried that not believing in hell is blasphemous and could land someone there all the more quickly.

I have found lately that the less I care about what other people think of me, the more they seem to care about what I think of them. I imagine that sounds cocky.

A part of me feels self-conscious about this book. It wants the book to be good and for you to think it is good (and to therefore think that I am good and smart and wise, etc.). Part of me thinks it could be better. Another part thinks that I shouldn't let "perfect" get in the way of "great." Some days I think the book will be huge, Oprah huge, and I wonder if my saying so makes that reality more or less likely. I showed an earlier draft to an agent and he said it was terrible. He even said that this confession section was no good. I'm not famous enough, he told me, and therefore no one will care about my confession, or, if they do care, it will only put them off. So maybe this book will be a total flop. Maybe I've already blown it by writing what I wrote above.

When I was younger the doctors diagnosed me with ADHD, Attention Deficit Hyperactive Disorder. They prescribed medicine in the hope of drowning out what they took to be an aberration of my spirit, but which I eventually realized was spirit. So I stopped taking it, gave myself a new diagnosis: Ambitious Defiant Happy Danimal (my nickname). I began to focus on what I could do, given my natural temperament, rather than what doctors told me I couldn't do. Ambitious Defiant Happy Danimal (or Attention Dialed into a Higher Dimension) is a story I tell myself as a reminder not to live by other people's expectations.

I actually think the doctor's diagnosis is a story too, a different story, based on similar facts. Their story assumes that because I seem less interested in certain details, or because I seem interested for a period of time that is shorter than what they consider "normal," that there is something wrong with me and I should take medicine to correct it. My story, on the other hand, assumes that the things that interest me are the things I'm meant to be interested in, and that if things don't interest me I choose not to force it.

Maybe it's not a matter of learning disorders, but of teaching disorders? Or maybe we can simply encourage people to do what they naturally want to, rather than try to make them normal? I could have accepted the doctor's diagnosis as a limiting belief, and rationalized to myself all the reasons why I couldn't write a book. But that would have been ignoring the part of me that wanted to write a book, the part that wanted to figure out how to do it most effectively based on who I am.

I love Jesus, Yeshua, and believe that He is my savior. Some of you, I imagine, will write me off because of that. You'll think I'm too religious, which is a nice way of saying "naive." Others of you, I imagine, will take issue with me invoking Jesus' name because you'll say I have no right to do so. "He's not Christian enough," you might say. "He's a heretic or blasphemer." Then there's those of you who might think I'm too new-agey, too surfer-ish, too bro-ish, too whatever.

My original design for this book was to have the confession on the very first page. I thought it would be an explosive and catchy beginning, and after all, it's one of the first exercises we do on retreats, usually after a polar plunge. Later, I decided not to confess first thing, because out of context maybe it's a bit too much. I choose to believe I made the best decision.

Why am I writing this book? I could tell you the reasons that I imagine would please you, but given the time constraint, and that this is a confession, I'll limit it to the more "negative" reasons that I am more resistant to sharing. I want people to take me seriously. I want to make money. I want to advance my career and make myself seem more important.

It's important to feel important. I imagine everyone wants to feel important. I think everyone alive is alive for a reason, and that makes them important. I'm important, though—as my higher Self reminds me—not more important than anyone else. My other self, however, calculates that if my goals are power, influence and fame, that kind of admission could be useful.

***

Having done this exercise dozens of times, I imagine that some of you, at least in part, weren't really listening to my confession, because you were busy preparing your own. You might have been thinking, calculating: "Of all the things I don't want to reveal, which ones am I willing to say, which ones will elicit a favorable reaction?" My brother Timothy is great at calling attention to this habit of preparation. On the one hand, he says, it takes us out of the present moment, so that we're not able to hear and feel what the other person is expressing, because we're up in our heads. On the other hand, he says, preparing ourselves is a form of protecting ourselves. This is a space in which to let go of protection. That's what the agreements are for.

After one person goes there are a few different ways to proceed. One is to simply have the next person go, rotating around the circle left or right. Another way is to wait in silence until someone else decides to speak up. One of my personal favorite ways is to have the person who just confessed ask someone else in the group a taboo question as a way of passing the torch. That person answers the question, and begins his or her confession.

I've noticed that a lot of people use a lot of their time with needless build up. Their confession comes wrapped in layers and layers of fat. There's often one "big" thing they want to reveal, but before they do so they cloak it in details and digressions and false starts. Maybe they think they're building tension by doing so, as a way of making their big reveal that much bigger, but more often than not, the opposite happens. They say the thing they didn't want to say, and the rest of us are like, "That's it? That's the thing you didn't want us to know? From all that buildup, we thought you were about to give us the nuclear codes." That's not to say that the thing they reveal isn't a big deal. It is a big deal to the person confessing, but the point I'm making is that the sooner they say it, the sooner they drop the backpack, and the sooner it stops holding them back. In addition to the thing they don't want to say are all the psychic fences they've built around it, all the conflicting layers of interpretation between them and the truth.

Before the next person goes there's one last thing. The more dangerous it feels to say the thing you don't want to say, the more your heart pounds at the prospect of saying it, the more important it is to say it, and the more freedom you have to gain by doing so. You'll know you're telling more of the truth when you start to doubt the things you say.

 *My earliest memories* (the next person begins) are of wetting the bed. I probably wet the bed two to three times a week well into elementary school. I even remember stealing one of my little sister's diapers and hiding it in the closet, years after I'd been potty trained, because I wanted to wear it.

I threw a rock at my dog once. She had stolen my sock and was running figure eights with it in the backyard. I felt angry and wanted to scare her and reassert my dominance, so I picked up a small rock. It was very small, probably not even—

"Story."

I threw it, not trying to hit her, but at the last minute she turned and the rock hit her square between the eyes. She yelped very loud, dropped the sock, and came and cowered at my feet.

The first woman I saw naked was my mom, and it's like the image of her was imprinted on my mind, so that every girl I dated I subconsciously measured against her. I even told one girl that her hair color was a turnoff because it wasn't the same as my mom's.

I quit the swim team when I was five years old because I was too embarrassed to wear a Speedo. I thought people would say I had a small penis.

The first time I masturbated was with a master lock. I locked it around my erection and moved it up and down until I ejaculated.

Between the ages of fifteen and seventeen I stole clothes from department stores.

The first chance I had to get it on with a girl I faked being sick because I was afraid she would think I was a terrible kisser. Years later, during spring break, I had a chance to have sex with an extremely hot girl. I blew it, because earlier I had eaten too much pizza and as we were making out I had to take a poo, so I left her hotel room, went back to mine (I couldn't bring myself to poop in her bathroom) but when I got there I found police outside my door.

Turns out, someone had reported noise and drugs and drinking, so the police detained me for questioning and eventually kicked me out of the hotel.

Nowadays I'm afraid that I'm not living up to my potential. I'm thirty years old and maybe I've missed the boat entirely and I'm destined to be a failure. Sometimes I think about my family and other important people in my life dying, and I even fantasize a little that such a tragedy would finally get me to stop procrastinating on my life.

When I was younger, I would stick a pillow between my legs and notice that it felt good. I would shift back and forth a little to rub myself on it. I didn't really know what I was doing, just that I really liked the way it felt. I got caught doing it once too. I was in the car with my family—we were on our way to church—and for some reason the way I was sitting hit the same spot as the pillow. My mom saw me fidgeting and told me to stop. I don't think she knew what I was doing, but I still felt embarrassed about it.

I have pleasured myself to things other than my boyfriend, and I am afraid that if I told him he would be upset and self-conscious and that it might cause problems in our relationship.

I read a lot of fan-fiction online, a lot, and I feel self-conscious about it because I think people judge it as stupid or escapist or whatever, and that they might say that the fact that I read it means my own life isn't romantic enough.

Sometimes I think my boyfriend is too controlling, and if I told my mom about it she might pressure me to break up with him.

I think about my ex-boyfriend sometimes, and wonder if I'd be better off with him.

I wonder if I'm a cold-hearted bitch sometimes because I don't feel more connected to my family. I enjoy spending time with them, but I'm also happy when it's time to go home and back to my own life.

I felt some shame in the past because when my baby was born I didn't feel love for it right away. It took a few weeks before I felt it. Even now sometimes it feels like I don't respond to her quickly enough. If we're around other people and she cries, people say "oh it breaks my heart to see her crying." But it doesn't break my heart. Not even when she's screaming. Should it? Should I be more upset when she cries? I don't think she's in pain, but maybe I'm not attuned enough. I felt horrible when I was trimming her nails and accidentally cut her. I feel guilty for being on my phone so much while I'm breastfeeding—for two reasons, one because it's like I'm not paying enough attention to her, and two because what if I'm harming her by having the phone so close.

I confess that I like hearing everyone else confess so that I can gauge how messed up I think they are. It makes me feel better to think they are worse off than me. But at the same time, while other people are confessing I rehearse and think about what it is that I want to confess. In that way, I have a hard time catching myself off guard and being spontaneous. It's like I can't get out of my own head. In fact, when other people talk to me, it seems like I'm listening only for the things they say that apply to me, and the rest I sort of discard. In that way, I think I'm very selfish. I'm listening for answers to questions I'm not sure I'm asking. I notice that I want you all to appreciate me and praise me and think I'm special, but I don't want to ask you directly for any of that, because I think that if I have to ask, then it isn't true or real. At all times, I need to know who I'm better than and who I'm worse than. I'm constantly ranking people and seeing what I can get out of them. And I don't know why, or how to stop it, or if I should stop it. I think I must have missed an important day in elementary school or something that would have taught me some basic lessons about being alive, because the way I am now, I'm not really sure of anything at all.

***

Some confessions are short and some are long. Sometimes it's a single detail that people both deeply desire to get off their chest and are afraid to get off their chest. Other times people meander around their confession with redundant details. By that I mean they tiptoe with their words around the thing they really want to say, either building it up or talking it down, all the while avoiding the thing directly. Their confession could be over in a matter of seconds, if they would just come out and say it.

"I used to put peanut butter on my balls and let my dog lick it off."

"I had sex with a cow once."

"I cheated my way through high school."

"I stole money from my friend."

"Sometimes I wonder if I married the wrong person, if I'd be better off either alone or with someone else."

"When I'm fighting with my wife, there is a voice inside me that wants me to push it, to say the meanest things I could possibly say as a way of testing her. Like, if the relationship breaks, it wasn't so solid to begin with."

"I let myself get fat and out of shape because I stopped wanting physical attention from my husband."

"I lie a lot. Like, a lot a lot. I'm probably lying and withholding right now."

"I'm a bad sister. At times when my siblings need me I run away. I don't want to deal with their problems or let them in on mine."

The purpose of confession isn't really the details of what's confessed. It's more about meeting and overcoming the resistance that keeps us from coming clean. It can be challenging (because we've made it challenging) to speak the blunt and honest truth. The question it raises is, *Where else in your life are you dancing around the main issue, and in what ways is that holding you back?* When you stop putting energy into resisting or hiding something that may or may not even be true, you get a surge of energy to do the things that make you feel good.

In fact, as more and more members of the group confess, it becomes difficult to keep track of who confessed what. It all starts to blend together, and you realize that everyone has things they feel shame about or have felt shame about, everyone has things they'd rather not say, things in their past that a part of them regrets having done. Those "personal" details, you see, are actually universal.

We're all in a bit of a pickle in our lives. We're all facing certain challenges. So much of our behavior is driven by unconscious motives. Confession is about bringing light to those motives, raising them consciously so they don't sabotage us in secret. It grounds you in the present moment and aligns you with yourself—or, at the very least, it alerts you to the ways you might not be aligned. Until you can talk about what you don't want to talk about, and say the things you're afraid to say, the things you won't even admit to yourself, I'm not sure you're ever free of the jail of your mind. Allow yourself to be transparent, and let the chips fall where they may. That's how you gain freedom from living up to other people's expectations, from the addiction to fitting in. The bridges you might burn, in my experience, will often light your way to greater opportunities.

As I alluded to earlier, it is said that a person is only as sick as his or her secret. The more it's held in, the sicker it can make one. There are countless people who have believed their thoughts were true simply because they kept them in for so long. In the vacuum of their own minds the stories make perfect sense, but exposed to the light and air of reality, that is, spoken aloud in complete sentences to an audience of listeners, the same secret that once seemed so true and so powerful now sounds silly, riddled with inconsistencies, or flat out wrong. I think that's why confession is at the foundation of so many religious, spiritual, and psychological practices, because it reveals the "truth" about such secrets: Namely, they're not so secret, and a lot of the time, they're pretty normal. What's most personal is most universal—and that realization is infinitely healing.

After years of confessions, I've yet to find a better, quicker way to get to know someone. It still gets my heart to pound, and gives me an immediate high on life. It's the most addicting drug I've tried.

This is not an invitation to word vomit anywhere and everywhere for the rest of your life. It is an invitation, right here, right now, in a safe context, to let go of filtering yourself, clear the crap out and detonate the landmines. It is an opportunity to short-circuit the mind's censor and peek into your own subconscious to see what's really down there. "How can I know what I think unless I see what I say?" This is the space to say it, to get it out. After it's out, then we can think and talk about it, we can sort out where it came from and what it means. Until it's out, though, it is, as you know, silently undermining you, because what you resist persists. For now, get it out.

Here is one thing I believe I know: if you feel sensations associated with fear at the prospect of coming clean, you probably have a lot to gain by doing so.

***

There is a part two to this exercise. Having gone to one extreme by confessing the things we don't want people to know about us, we now go to the opposite extreme, by saying all the things we do want people to know about us. We call this the narcissism portion of the exercise. Given our history of dimming our light in front of others, this portion of the exercise is about shining it brighter than we normally feel comfortable. It's a reversal of the cultural conditioning we have about being modest.

In one minute or less, say the things you do want people to know about you—but exaggerate them, even brag. Try to sound more confident than you really are.

For example…

"I am very good at telling the truth, probably better than most people I know. I catch myself in dishonesty quicker than others, which makes me that much more honest. I am a great listener. I hear what people say, but more than that, I hear what they don't say. I know parts of them better than they know themselves. I can tell by listening how congruent they are with what they say. I can listen to the way a person talks about someone else and get a pretty good idea of the way they think about themselves. I see through the matrix and glean your true potential. I allow you to feel important in my presence. I show you the courage to get *funcomfortable* and change your life. I have a vision not only for what is, but for what could be. I am strong and limber and athletic. I can surf, hike, run, lift, and fight. My right hook can knock people out. I get paid to play. My job is my life and my life is my job. I am always working, never working. My life is a constant vacation because I am willing to take risks and leaps of faith."

Other examples…

"I am amazing at meditation and sparking people to see things about themselves they've never seen before. I look really great in blue. I am the best personal trainer in history because I am similar to Bruce Lee—that is, I combine all modalities to create the super modality."

"I'm a master alchemist and I can tell every one of you what your biggest problem is just by looking at you."

"I am smarter than most people I meet. They are operating at one or maybe two levels, but I see all the levels all at once. I have experienced what the mystics talk about, the vision of everything connected. I know why the world is the way it is. I know exactly why. It is beyond words. I believe that I should be paid simply for who I am. The thoughts in my head are enough for a Nobel Prize, and one day, everyone's gonna know it."

***

Here are four things to hold onto when doing the Confession exercise:

1) A joy shared is a joy doubled.

2) A sorrow shared is a sorrow halved.

3) There is one person who can shine light on your shadows, and that is you.

4) Being bold enough to express things you are scared to share can set you free.

***

It's worth mentioning the experience of being in the audience. The healing takes place in both the person on stage and in the others watching. What it is, I believe, is yet another opportunity for us in the audience to see ourselves in other people, to realize that everyone is a mirror reflecting back to us. We see in other people what we are, what we want, or what we don't like about ourselves. If there's a certain quality you can point to in another person, it's because you possess that quality yourself to a greater or lesser degree. That aggression and power you notice about such and such guy—that's your aggression, your power. The anger you see is your anger. The beauty you see is your beauty. Whatever it is, it's yours in some capacity. Otherwise you wouldn't notice it. The tenderness is yours. The defensiveness is yours. The humor is yours. The intelligence, yours. The nervousness, yours.

Not every confession is a home run, for a lot of reasons. Not knocking it out of the park, though, by no means makes a failure. Confession takes practice. Each time you do it is a little different. I haven't felt the same way after every confession I've ever done. Sometimes after doing it I'll notice myself thinking about it a few hours later, and I'll realize that there were other things I wanted to confess more than the things I actually did confess. I'll reflect on this and see what it brings up for me, and then I'll appreciate it as an opportunity to learn and a symptom that I'm still growing. Frankly, it seems to happen that some people, sometimes, have things to reveal that are more controversial than others, things they've been resisting and putting a lot of energy into, which makes their confessions that much more explosive. Everything is an experience. It's always a learning opportunity. Explosive or not, when someone is going for it, really digging in and revealing some things they don't want known, they're spellbinding to watch. We can't take our eyes off of them. It's a crazy paradox: by saying the things they think will cause them to be ridiculed and excluded, they get our full, undivided attention, and sometimes our applause.

At the end of the exercise we say the following words, quoted from Fritz Perls:

> *I do my thing, and you do your thing. I am not in this world to live up to your expectations, and you are not in this world to live up to mine. You are you, and I am I. If by chance we find each other, it is beautiful. If not, it can't be helped.*

I believe it can be helped...by *breaking normal.*

If the first sign of shame is hiding, the first step out of shame is not hiding.

Chapter 6

Feature Your Flaws

Disclaimer: I've facilitated this exercise a handful of times in the mixed company of men and women. As my wife's and my REALationship evolved, we currently feel complete with this particular exercise. We no longer practice this at our events either.

With that said, given how much I believe in the liberating power of this exercise and the miraculous transformations I've seen through this process, I feel it is integral for me to include this section for you to decide how it may or may not fit into your healing. For a final hearts-up, this process has the ability to catalyze immense amounts of suppressed emotions to surface in a heartbeat. If you feel the call to participate or facilitate, consider starting with a group of your same sex, and/or teaming up with professionals that understand the depth of what this can bring up.

* * *

What better way to follow up this progression of *baring all* than to actually get naked?

This exercise might be a one-offer, something you do just once in your life and reap the benefits of for the rest of your days. Like the other exercises, the genius is in its simplicity: we get naked and look at each other's bodies, and after a while, we talk about them.

I've seen the shyest, most timid and insecure of people transform in under five minutes. I've seen the light come back in their eyes. I've seen women cry and shake and struggle to take off their clothes, as though invisible shackles were preventing them from doing so, only to jump around naked and ecstatic moments later.

From inside the matrix this probably sounds crazy or perverted. It's a good thing, then, that we're not in the matrix, but rather on the path of discovery. To us, "crazy" is a compliment, because what commonly goes by "normal" is from another perspective, pretty absurd. What is perverted about something we all share in common? We all have bodies, there's no way around it. So why should it be normal to feel shame about them, or to think there's something wrong with them (meaning there's something wrong with us) if they don't look a certain way? Why is it normal to put so much energy into neurotically hiding our bodies from other people, dressing up in order to fit in? If we all have butts and we all go poop, why are we so compulsively private about it, sneaking away to do it out of sight, and covering our scent up afterward? Why, if we all have penises and vaginas, does typing those words bring up some resistance in me, as I imagine reading those words brings up some resistance in you?

"So you're promoting nudism?"

We are not promoting nudism, nor are we condemning it. We are leveraging a taboo our culture has around the body in order to awaken the spirit that lives within it, or, in some cases, the spirit that is trapped within it. Some of us got so hung up in the past on our physical appearance and games of comparison that we wrecked our self-confidence and became alienated from ourselves. The sooner we get over all that, the sooner we get out of our own way.

If the first sign of shame is hiding, the first step out of shame is not hiding. For Adam and Eve that means removing the fig leaves and stepping out of the shadows. For us it means taking our clothes off, wiping away the masks and makeup, and exposing the parts of our bodies we are most self-conscious about. If you can't put your naked self out there, how will you put your work or ideas out there, how will you accept and promote yourself if you think yourself is something that needs to be hidden, covered up, or packaged appropriately according to the likes and dislikes of others?

Rarely is anyone "ready" for this exercise. As soon as we announce it people seem to get jittery.

"Now? We're going to do it right now? But..."

Yes. Right now.

No one is required to participate, but even the skeptics linger. A part of their mind is sounding the alarm, telling them to run and hide. Another part is curious, and says wait a minute. After all, how often do we have the opportunity to see a bunch of strangers naked in real life? How often do we see anyone naked in our day to day life, especially in a non-pornographic, non-sexual way? How often do we get naked in front of others?

For a lot of us the answer is never, or at least not for a long time, since the innocence of our early years. Maybe we catch a glimpse of our own nakedness, for a hot second before and after our morning shower, but after that it's into a uniform based on our social function or some image we want to project. The uniform reinforces a Function Based Identity, or FBI.

The naked exercise is effective because the mere mention of it, even before the clothes come off, produces a litany of feelings. Everything from flushed cheeks to queasy stomachs to chattering teeth. Some people begin to shake. Others, feeling the sudden urge to pee, sneak away out of sight. Our palms sweat, our hearts pound.

It's a scary step. Many people are insecure about their bodies, almost as if they're ashamed to have one. They worry that people will judge. They worry they are ugly, fat, flawed, pasty, pimply, dark, different, abnormal, and overall undesirable. As a man, having just gotten out of cold water, you might think your manhood will appear smaller than normal. As a woman, you might feel acutely self-conscious of your "problem areas," and, having internalized years of commercials and magazines, tell yourself they make you less beautiful. But either way, man or woman, it can be scary to reveal yourself in front of others. What will they think of you, based on your human bodysuit? Will they judge you as ugly or unworthy? Will they reject you or make fun of you?

To be naked in front of other people is to let them see you as you are, rather than who you pretend to be. A lot of us fear that who we are is too much or not enough.

Those fears are not bad. They heighten the contrast, raise your awareness, and give the exercise more power. It's about observing those fears, feeling them, and going forward anyway. That's how you find freedom. Just like polar plunging, you can breathe deep and still get in the water, or in this case, naked.

The first time I did it the amount of adrenaline pumping through my body made me feel like I could flip a car. I felt cold and shaky and yet, like everyone else, I tried to stand there nonchalant. What I noticed, though, was that the harder we all tried to act natural, the funnier and more foolish we actually looked. There we were, butt naked among strangers we'd only recently met, averting our eyes from one another, but reluctantly; interested, but trying to act like we weren't. All we really wanted to do was check out everyone's body, especially their private parts, to see what they were like compared with ours. Within about five seconds of having our clothes off, we had made a map of these comparisons and ranked ourselves among them.

It's interesting. As long as we had clothes on we could talk and laugh and interact with one another. We could do handstands and give hugs or high fives. As soon as the clothes came off, however, as soon as we got naked, suddenly we could barely look at one another—it felt, somehow, weird…For a full minute it was quiet and what some might call awkward. No one spoke. No one made eye contact. We didn't look because, well, we couldn't see. Our vision was clouded with the pictures our minds projected, stories of our flaws and inadequacies. Literally, we couldn't get over ourselves.

For me those flaws start (ahem, started) with my feet. They're flat. In the past I thought they were ugly, and I was self-conscious about showing them to other people. They kind of look like hobbit feet and, I guess I thought they made me look unathletic or something. Next were my legs, which were always strong but didn't look like what I associated with strength. They're skinny and bowed out. I used to think they made me look goofy. (If I still do think that, I tell myself that goofy is a great thing.) Above my legs, my butt. Like my feet, it's also a little flat. A part of me used to wish, and maybe still does, that my butt was bigger, more rounded and muscular, like the kind of butts I see on billboards.

I was never really worried or self-conscious about my penis. My chest, though, that's an area where I used to compare myself to other people. My pecs are ripped and have great definition, but I used to think they were too rounded, and maybe a little soft looking. Sometimes, from the right (or wrong) angle, they looked like manboobs.

These "problem" areas dominated my attention in those first couple minutes, and I think the same was true for the rest of the group. The urge to cover up and hide was strong, but paradoxically, the thing that kept us from doing so was exactly the thing we were there to get over: concern for what other people think of us. As excited as we were to be liberated from over-caring how others see us, we didn't want to be seen as weak or quitters.

After a while we seemed to grow out of it enough to at least look in the direction of others. We felt our curiosity rising. As it did it ran into another layer of so-called awkwardness and discomfort. Sure, we could look in their general direction, but could we really observe and see them? The awkwardness, again, was the thing we were there to get over. We wanted to see (of course we wanted to see) but we didn't want other people to see we wanted to see. We didn't want to appear to be too interested. Instead of honestly and unabashedly looking, then, we stole quick glances before returning our gaze to eye-level. It was this weird, restrictive energy that seemed to control us so long as it remained unsaid. Thankfully my brother (who is great at sharing his vulnerability) called it out, named the elephant, meaning he said aloud the thing we were all thinking but not saying. We laughed because we knew it was true. Afterward, our curiosity rose even higher. We felt freer, more at ease, able to look around, reflect, appreciate one another.

I'm imagining right now that there are some readers whose minds go immediately to sex (maybe because a part of my mind goes immediately to sex), and therefore think the exercise is inherently sexual, but that's not the case. If your mind jumps to sex it might be because you're preoccupied with sex, which might mean you're in resistance to it—which isn't a bad thing, but it is something to notice and be aware of, rather than jump unwittingly to projected conclusions. The less you're aware of it, as I'll say again and again, the more it exercises control over you.

***

With that said, one guy got an erection, and having no pants to tuck it under, he sat there with it more or less on display. What could he do? "Should" he have felt shame about it? "Should" we? There's this impulse to immediately label and categorize and file it away, but checking that impulse allowed him and us the chance to sit there with our feelings and thoughts about it. Is anything else more natural? How can we be sure that getting an erection is weirder than not getting one, or that the "weirdness" isn't our own projection? So just like with the initial restrictive energy against looking, rather than ignore the erection and let it become an unspoken elephant in the room, we called attention to it. We acknowledged what was happening, accepted it, and moved through it. We made fun of it, not in a malicious way, but literally—we made it fun, *funcomfortable*, that is.

"I notice your erection, and I imagine…"

The point of the exercise—like the point of this book and life—is whatever you make it. For me it was a mirror, and a mirror shows you what your mind wants to see. A part of my mind wanted to see sex, but another part wanted to see comparison and critique, the way I subconsciously critiqued myself. Still another part, which I tend to consider deeper than the previous two, saw similarities. I realized that looking at a group of naked people is almost the same as looking at a group of clothed people: from head to toe there are differences and variations, but regardless, say, of what color top a person is wearing, you still recognize it as a shirt. Similarly, no matter what shape someone is, or what their butt looks like, you still recognize them as human. We all look a little different to tell each other a part. As many people as there are, there are that many different ears, belly-buttons, genitals, knees, hips and elbows. There is no standard for how we should all look, no cookie cutter that we should fit, and no justification, none whatsoever, for statements like, "this person is more attractive than that person." At most, at the very most, you can say, "this person is more attractive to me than that person" or "from my perspective, so and so looks closer to the image on the front covers of certain magazines than someone else." It's a way of comparing that doesn't force you to choose one over the other. To my mind that's a truer interpretation of reality. It is appreciating difference, not ironing it out.

Attraction is funny. Sometimes we're attracted to unexpected things, which exercises like this one make clear. You might find that the people you think you're going to be attracted to or who you tell yourself you "should" be attracted to aren't the same ones you feel attracted to once the clothes come off. Should and shouldn't, however, are concepts of the mind, whereas attraction, like inspiration, is a full-body function of the heart, body, mind and soul. Like the spontaneous erections mentioned above, that attraction is the physiological equivalent of inspiration—and a lot of people have made a habit in the past of ignoring it, because according to this type of dominating, self-fulfilling story they tell themselves, that inspiration came from somewhere it "shouldn't" have, and is lower, or worse, or less than a rational, logical, or ultra-spiritual mindset.

Think about it: erections aren't deliberate. They don't necessarily happen because we consciously will them to. Arousal, for the most part, might be beyond our conscious control, and to feel shame about it reflects our deepest attitude toward ourselves.

This is one of the unintended benefits of the exercise: to stop ignoring the things that speak to you. In accepting whatever it is that inspires or attracts or arouses you, you accept the parts of yourself—perhaps your deepest parts—that are inspired and attracted and aroused. Those are the parts you're afraid of, not your "flaws" and not your "weaknesses." You're afraid of those parts because they lead to your hidden strengths, which take you to places you haven't even imagined yet, beyond the limits in your head. Instead of building inspiration around your so-called life, that is, "when it happens to fit in," build life around your inspiration, and have the faith to go where it leads you.

***

The second part of the exercise is standing front and center.

More alarms go off. More feelings race through you. Good feelings, because remember, they're all good, so long as you feel them. You observe the alarms, observe the feelings, and breathe through them, play with them, make them fun.

This is probably the most vulnerable moment of the exercise, and the rarest thing of all is for a person to volunteer to go first, and then walk up, turn around, stand perfectly still and meet the audience's gaze. More likely, the urge to hide kicks into overdrive. Eventually someone goes first. Someone has to go first. Since I've already "shown" you my body above, let's give someone else a chance. Let's say it's a woman. Let's say she's 5'6" and 140 pounds (Are you judging based on that information alone?).

You would think that standing naked front and center is as naked and exposed as someone can get. But then there's that outer armor, that shield of muscle and skin. This woman, you notice, is still trying to hide. Her shoulders are slumped, her skin seems flexed. She's curled inward, taking very shallow breaths, barely filling her lungs. It's as if she's trying to appear small and inconsequential, or so you imagine. She crosses her arms, maybe to cover her belly or chest. Or maybe she talks a lot and exaggerates her hand gestures as a way of distracting our eyes. You notice that she's turned at an angle, not quite giving us a full frontal, as if she's avoiding letting us see her thighs or hips. You notice that she moves side to side, making herself a moving target. Rather than meet our gaze, she looks down at her own body as though she's dissociating from it, trying to identify herself with us as examiners, as others.

In other words, she's squirming, as if under a magnifying glass. She's visibly nervous, maybe on the verge of tears. Logically, she knows she's naked and that we can see everything, and that for her to stand at an angle only calls our attention to whatever it is she might be hiding. The question, then, is who is she hiding from? The answer, I believe, is herself, her inner critic, which, more likely, is an internalized critic: her mother, a friend from school, a celebrity, a billboard, a magazine, etc.

Somewhere along the way, many places along the way, she's listened to a serpent that told her she was flawed and unattractive, that convinced her that the value of who she was as a person, as a soul, could somehow be measured by the appearance of her body. We might say it's all in her head, but in reality, it's not that easy. Subconsciously she's become identified with her body, and that low self-worth is both a refuge and a trap. A refuge because she figures that if she's not worth anything she can therefore do nothing—so why try anything at all? Better to stay put and accept her lot. A trap because, when you ask her to turn her hips and reveal what she wants to conceal, it's almost as if she can't, as if physically she can't perform the motion. There is nothing external restraining her, but the resistance has taken over on the inside, and confines her with invisible shackles. For her to turn her hips requires such exertion, such force of will, such letting go (I've seen this happen) that her body shakes, even though from the outside there's nothing holding her back.

It's not so much that she doesn't want us to see it. She knows we can see it. It's that she doesn't want to see us see it, because as long as that's the case she subconsciously has an out, which prevents her from having to identify and own it. Energetically, she shifts away from it. She doesn't want to go near her thighs, doesn't even want to acknowledge them. That whole area is physically and emotionally quarantined, off limits, making her a prisoner in her own skin.

I think what's happening in this woman is that the self-defeating stories are breaking down. The internalized critic knows that once she turns her hips and sees the group doesn't flat-out reject her as a person, then that critic is dead in the water, and she can take back the other things it has claimed. Outward shaking is evidence of internal struggle. Our role as observers is to encourage her in that struggle.

She will likely hide her face when she finally turns to face us, but eventually she'll look up and watch us for a reaction, to see how we're taking it, how we're taking her. She's imagined our reaction many times already, and that imagination is based off reactions she received in the past from parents, peers, or even herself. But really, she's the one doing it. She's the one doing the seeing and judging in the mirror of her own mind. In the past, she experienced something that she imagined was judgment, and on some level, she judged that judgment to be correct and internalized it. Now, judgment is what she looks for. Her self-talk is ridicule. Shame and scorn are what she expects.

I imagine she is surprised, then, when she looks up and meets our gaze. As she watches us watch her, as she sees us see her, she feels what we feel and sees what we see. It's not negative judgment. It's not a focus on her flaws. We're naked too, and preoccupied by our own vulnerability. More importantly, we've realized that this part of the exercise is about us as much as it is about her. The healing in both places is simultaneous.

In the audience, you realize that if you aren't struck by the beauty of her bravery, by the sheer display of emotions, the rawness of her, it might be an indication that you don't yet accept your own bravery, your own emotions and rawness, and that you're still trying to hide and avoid yourself.

You see that the more she tries to hide certain parts of herself, the more obvious those parts are. That can catalyze you to think about the parts of yourself that you try to hide. In the past, you may have looked for the flaws in other people in order to give yourself the peace of writing them off. Curiously enough, that's exactly how you treated yourself: looking in the mirror, you consciously or subconsciously criticized every little thing, tried to write yourself off so that you could continue to play it safe and small. But now you see: "flaws" don't discredit people; they endear people. You wouldn't throw someone away because they're different, or "imperfect," so why throw away yourself? Ultimately, in looking at her, you realize you're looking at yourself, and that any judgments that come up about her are a reflection of the ones you hold within.

What happens next is hard to describe. As we in the audience hold the space, all that restrictive energy dissipates. She slips into a strangely new, strangely familiar suit—her own body. Our presence, bearing witness, allows her to re-claim herself—"flaw" by "flaw," problem area by problem area. By exposing the things she wants to hide, she becomes less self-conscious about those things, and they cease to weigh down her psyche. Right before our eyes she acknowledges and accepts the areas she internally resisted and shut down. She slides past the invisible quarantine, taming, mastering the part of herself that in the past cared so much what other people thought of her, that it convinced her to hide who she was. As she becomes more open and aligned, she visibly relaxes, her body loosens up, and the tension she was holding goes slack. Her spine straightens, her breath deepens—and you might notice you feel more attracted to her than you did a moment ago. No surprise there. She stopped dimming her light.

Our deepest Self desires to be known, because in the beginning it lived naked and unashamed. It knows that true freedom lives in vulnerability, and it craves the boundlessness of not hiding.

You are more than your body. The way to realize it is to reveal it. Not to read about it, not to think about it, and not to say you "should" know better—but to do it.

*REALationships are based on
open curiosity rather than
secret condemnation.*

Chapter 7

Team "Dianiel"

I met my wife on a retreat in upstate New York. My brothers and I had hosted many retreats by then, and as the "RawBrahs" we'd been posting videos to YouTube for a few years. Unbeknown to me, this young woman, Diana Hansen, who lived in Denmark—a country I'd never been to—had been watching those videos. Like a lot of our fans, or so I imagine, her life was in a rut of some sort and she was looking for that catalyst for freedom and change. She thought, judging from our videos, that we were ridiculous and crazy brothers who traveled all over and probably fooled around with a lot of girls. Nonetheless, some of the things we talked about didn't seem all that crazy. In fact, they seemed pretty accurate, pretty honest. Self-acceptance through self-expression, honoring yourself before the opinions and agendas of other people, and letting go of our attachment to destinations in favor of waking up to the dream of life unfolding now. These things resonated with her, and she could hear the truth of these messages through a lot of the otherwise "crazy" things we did. So, after following us on social media for a few months, when the pain of action became less painful than that of inaction, she decided to reach out to us to ask about our next retreat.

The cost alone almost stopped her from coming, along with the logistics of travel. Against the advice of many of her friends and family (who didn't understand the appeal of the RawBrahs), she made it happen. In three days, she sold most of what she owned, packed up the rest, stored it at a friend's, and booked ticket to Albany, New York.

I'd hosted enough retreats by then to know that it's a good idea to delay making definitive judgments about people based on their social media profiles, because I'd found that the way people presented themselves on Facebook was not always the way they appeared in real life. Sometimes I'd meet a guy or girl at the airport, someone I'd emailed and checked out on Facebook, and hardly recognize them.

With Diana that wasn't the case. I was attracted to her right away, and thanks to the context of our retreats, I didn't have to beat around the bush in expressing that attraction. Our first real talk was a confession. Within the course of a few hours I had learned from her a version of the story of her life—the version she was most resistant to sharing. She received from me a similar version about my life, and the two of us were then free to share our judgments about the stories we'd heard. We didn't tell each other the things we wanted to say, or the things we wanted to hear. We revealed the things about ourselves we didn't want each other to know about, the things we thought might sabotage any potential relationship we might have. I told her I didn't think she was marriage material because she wasn't a Christian, and she told me she couldn't stand the way I seemed to question everything. The moment before we confessed such judgments, I imagine we took them seriously, possibly as deal-breakers. The moment after confessing them, however, we realized that our judgments divided us so long as they remained unexpressed, but that expressing them made us feel more deeply connected. The bridges we burned, so to speak, lit the way forward.

We skipped what might have been months or even years of normal dating, by allowing ourselves to be seen for who we are—raw, authentic, literally and metaphorically naked.

Six months later—six divinely hectic, travel-filled months—I proposed to her on April Fool's. Those months were a real trial period, filled with road trips, long nights, fatigue, inspiration, differing schedules, missed connections that catalyzed other connections, and all the joy and stress that comes from embarking on a journey with a potential partner.

I can't recommend travel enough as a way of test-driving a new relationship, especially when you go to places and countries that neither of you have been to before. It gives you the opportunity to challenge each other and be challenged in each other's presence. It allows you to observe yourself through your partner's eyes as you react to new situations, and it allows you to observe your partner as he or she does the same. I got food poisoning in Peru and spent the night on and off the toilet—too sick to even think about hiding my "grossness" from her. She drank too much one night and performed an in-person equivalent of drunk dialing—that is, face to face, without the convenient distance afforded by a phone. Wanting to take care of each other and sit with each other in our hour of seeming desperation was a clue that we were committed to each other in a more than superficial way.

The very next day after I proposed, we got married at the Orange County courthouse in southern California. I wore Vibram Five-Fingers; she wore pink shorts and a tank top. Four years later she and I are still together, still growing, still traveling together literally and figuratively. We're on a permanent retreat with each other, a permanent holiday, living where we want to live and doing what we want to do. It's a grand adventure of life together rather than a blind or reluctant adherence to a socially acceptable itinerary of how a relationship "should" go. The only outcome we are almost attached to is co-creating a dream.

***

It was late evening in Encinitas, California, and the lights in our living room made some spots glow brighter than others. From our computer in the corner there came into the room the sound of chanting Buddhist monks, deep, resonant vibrations that filled the air around us. Diana was on the couch and I was beside her, the midwife in position between her legs. The two assistants moved about the room making preparations. The tub in the center was filled with warm water, ready for us to get in.

To this day, I can only imagine from the outside what Diana was going through, what deep stores of energy she must have been tapping into as she went through labor. Like running a marathon after a marathon. We were in the water, we were out of the water. Diana was sweating one minute, cold the next. Most of the time she remained in her trance, blacked out, in a way, so focused on the things happening in her body that she had little attention left for anything else.

Late in the evening, in the lamplit living room, there came a sort of crescendo, where everything rushed suddenly together—the chanting monks, the birthing tub, the midwife and two assistants, the windows separating the night outside. It wasn't lucidity, but overwhelming experience. The veil of life and death, pain and pleasure, was never thinner. At the moment Diana surrendered, gave up, it seemed, Divina, our daughter, came through.

Yes, we were co-creating a dream.

* * *

The foundation of this "real-ationship" is intimacy, which I think of as "into me you see." It means direct communication about the things I do and don't want to say, and a willingness to hear Diana say things she does and doesn't want to say.

This practice can apply to all relationships, not only the romantic kind. The coming chapters will present exercises by which we can hack the rat race of so-called regular relationships, and transform them into REALationships.

To the degree that one fears judgment from others is the degree to which one judges others.

Chapter 8

Judge Your Judgments

I n the past, whenever we met a new person, we tried first to demonstrate that we were normal, not crazy or weird or whacko.

We said things and did things we thought would win that person over, and if we were right, we formed a relationship. Then and only then did we reveal our weirdness piece by piece, hoping it wasn't weird enough to break the superficial bond we'd created. Not being sure of ourselves, we looked for reassurance from others. We put out feelers in all directions and monitored our social radar for potential threats and allies.

What we didn't know is that the same script we ran on others, they ran on us. The script was unconscious, unspoken, below the radar, and for that reason it ran the show.

That's the rat race of regular relationships. People half in the closet, half out, trying to manipulate each other into desired results; subconsciously acting out their own agendas. REALationships are based on open curiosity rather than secret condemnation. They are about locating each other on our individual journeys, finding synchronicities among moving targets, and catalyzing us to uncover who we really are.

"What's your name? Where are you from? What do you do?" When I hear these questions I actually hear deeper ones underneath: *What can I judge you for? How can I make myself feel more significant in your presence? What are your initial impressions of me? What don't you want me to know about you?*

It's pretty fun to play around with asking these questions directly instead of indirectly. In the so-called normal world, there's this idea that we shouldn't judge other people, based on the proposition that "who are we to do so?" Only God who is above, who sees all and hears all, can be trusted to be pure and good in His and/or Her evaluation. We forget that one of the most respected positions in society is that of a *judge*. Like God, like kings on the throne, judges sit in the courtroom higher than the lawyers and plaintiffs and defendants. They sit higher than the jury. They wear solemn robes and retreat to private chambers before issuing a ruling. If judging others was so bad, why is it that our law and order depends on it? In reality, judges are regular people who we've dressed up, people who we ourselves have judged to have good judgment, people we have judged to be wise, and therefore we put them in a position of authority. We invented judges so that they could provide something we crave: perspective, which leads to closure, which leads to peace and reconciliation.

Good judgment is essential to our lives and fundamental to our survival. It's hardwired into our brains, which adapted to make distinctions and evaluations quickly based on different factors. Without judging that a cave lion is different from a cave wall, for example, our distant ancestors would not have survived very long. We wouldn't be here today if—insisting on non-judgment—we failed to see the distinction between, say, predator and prey, or different types of plants, or clean and contaminated water.

The difference now is that it's not as obviously useful to us for survival as it was in the past. Today, when our basic needs are more easily met through technology, when the same tried and true foods are available in abundance, it would seem that we can get away without judging. But that's not really how it works. Judgment is divinely designed into us so we can survive. We judge continuously, even in our dreams. We do it while crossing the street. We do it while interacting with new groups of people. We do it every time we take a bite of food. We do it every time we select a potential partner. It's part of our inner monologue. To judge is to distinguish ourselves from something else as a way of maintaining our bodily integrity, our sense of identity. We are able to judge because we are different, and we are different so that we can judge. Besides, what we normally call non-judgment is a judgment.

As long as we're alive we're going to judge and be judged. The degree to which we're afraid of being judged might be the degree to which we ourselves judge others. Some of the least honest people I've met claim never to lie, and some of the most judgmental never to judge. Personally, I've found a lot of freedom in being more open and transparent about it.

***

In light of all this, there's a sort of upgraded ice-breaker we do, similar to the confession session but less formal. Instead of sitting in a circle, the exercise has everyone in the group mingle freely with the goal of meeting everyone, except that when they meet a new person, the questions they are inspired to ask are a bit different from the ones we might normally ask. These questions are designed to break the norm, and snap us out of any cultural conditioning or hypnosis.

Initially, they might cause people to be taken aback or shake their heads, but after that initial *funcomfort*, I find they elicit greater authenticity.

What can I judge you for? I think that's a great lead off question. Slightly taboo, but intuitively right. It seems daring to ask aloud, because it's off script and you have no idea what the other person is going to say. The question means, how can I differentiate myself from you, what markers can I use to put myself in relation to you? There's your name, of course, also your work and origin. But then again there's also your religion, your talents and hobbies, even your hair, your eyes, your color, size and shape. Naturally I'm judging these things too, subconsciously, at lightning speed with seemingly little conscious effort.

It's amazing how quickly "What can I judge you for?" gets to the heart of a connection, where two people allow themselves to be vulnerable to one another, and accept each other precisely for those vulnerabilities. "Show me your weak spots," it asks, "or the spots that you imagine to be weak, and which you therefore might try to hide." It could take years, I imagine, for casual acquaintances, friends, or even families to get to such a depth.

How can I make myself feel important around you? This is a question I imagine we are asking all the time without really asking it. It seems to me that as we're feeling out new people and situations, we are looking for openings in the conversation in which we can interject ourselves and what we consider to be our gifts. After the initial judgment or assessment of another person, we usually want to know where our strengths lie in relation to him or her. Being more expert in something at which someone else is a novice allows us to feel more important. How can I make myself feel important around you? This raises the question, do I want to feel important around you, and why or why not? The answers to that question, I imagine, will reveal a lot.

There are so many questions you can ask a person, which in my opinion catalyze a connection far quicker than the standard interview. In this exercise, we can play around with asking *funcomfortable* questions and hearing *funcomfortable* answers, because we've created a context of acceptance and honesty. Keep in mind, this is an exercise to be done among willing participants. Even though the more you practice this exercise the more adept you will become at breaking normal in your daily life, this is not a license to say whatever you want to whomever you want wherever you happen to see them. I don't advise or encourage you to go up to any random person at the grocery store and let loose with whatever comes to mind. To me that might be an abuse not only of this exercise, but to you and the other person.

Other questions include:

When was the first time you knew you were a sexual being?

What question do you not want to ask me?

What are your initial impressions of me?

When was the last time you had sex?

Do you have any history of addiction, infidelity, or STDs?

Truly illuminating questions are infinitely available, so be sure to create your own. And please do notify us at **BreakingNormal.com** and check in regularly for the questions we are adding to our database.

***

The next exercise we do is two-part: *sharing our judgments*, and *judging our judgments*.

Depending on how long we've suppressed judgments in our own lives, part one of this exercise can be a challenge. Expressing judgment about another person *to that person* is not a skill a lot of us are particularly adept at. Too often in the past we expressed our judgments as a form of condemnation. That's not the goal here. I trust that the exercises up to now—in particular the *Confession* and *Notice vs Imagine*—have brought to light the notion that everyone we meet is on a journey that we usually know very little about, and that most of the time, our judgments about them are based on partial information. We are always noticing things, and those things spark our imaginations, which then construct a story about what we've noticed, and those stories are often judgments of some sort—rankings of higher and lower, better or worse, desirable or not. It is thanks to our brain's constant activity that judgments spring up, almost without our willing them. The goal of sharing the judgment, then, is to shed light on it, to get it out of our heads so that it doesn't distract us from being present in the moment. The instinct to withhold judgment in the past might have come from a good place, but it caused the judgment to persist and run on repeat. It's like noticing a booger on the tip of someone else's nose, *not* saying something about it, and then being distracted by it for the rest of the conversation.

So, here's how the exercise goes. We sit in a circle, and invite anyone with a judgment about someone in the group to express it to that person.

"Travis, I have been judging you for your body. I judged you to be vain and superficial because your appearance always seems perfect to me."

"Andrea, I judged you earlier for your hair, specifically the way you've dyed it black. Your nails are black too, and the judgment I had was that you are not a Christian, and possibly you worship the devil."

"Kelly, I judged you for not going in the water, like you're afraid to be alive or feel anything that's not a neutral or positive sensation. It seems as if you want everything to be happy go lucky, which I judge to be shallow."

"Graham, I judge you for trying too hard."

"James, I observed myself judging you for the way you were talking to Stephanie, like you were trying to take advantage of her vulnerability."

The second part of the exercise is where we turn the mirror back on ourselves, by judging our own judgments. I remember my dad saying that if you have a problem with someone, you are the problem. It seems to me that the things we are most reluctant to admit about ourselves we tend to look for in other people. We judge and condemn them as a way of exonerating ourselves. The news is full of such examples: public declarations of homophobia from men still in the closet; condemnations of infidelity by people who have cheated or want to cheat themselves; bullies being bullied in the name of self-righteousness. On and on. For that reason, I've found it to be immensely healing to include this second step, which involves thinking about what our judgments really say about us who hold them, instead of doubling down on our own projections as a way of hiding in our shadows.

"I imagine, Travis, that I judged you for your body because a part of me envies it. Actually, I think I might judge you for it as a way of excusing myself for not working harder or eating healthier. Because if it's superficial and vain to have a nice body, then I get a free pass for being what I judge to be out of shape."

"Andrea, my judgment that you're not a Christian but possibly a devil worshiper, reflects, I believe, the parts of myself that are insecure about my own faith."

"Kelly, I think I judged you for not going in the water because I didn't really want to go in myself. I did it though, because I didn't want to be seen as a wuss. I judged you for not going in the water, but really I think I admire you for honoring yourself instead of the opinions of others."

"Graham, I judge you for trying too hard because sometimes I think I don't try hard enough. I try not to try, so that if I fail at something, or if it doesn't turn out how I wanted it to, I can say 'Oh well, I wasn't trying anyway.'"

"James, I think my judgment about you might hide a bit of envy, because I'm attracted to Stephanie and I want her to pay attention to me."

Sharing judgments in the interest of growth and connection is different from sharing them in the interest of being right. For that reason, when the judgments are out in the open, we let them sit there, and see what comes up. Sometimes the people who weren't on the receiving end of any judgment are the most triggered, and they are quick to jump out in defense of the person judged. To me this means simply that they have a judgment about the judger, which is pretty normal and natural, and we encourage them to share that judgment too. It's a group meditation and prayer, where the goal is to observe what comes up without getting attached to it and wrapped up in it.

Lastly, if someone is being vague in their judgment, if the group imagines that the person is pulling their punches or not getting to the root, it's important to call them up. It's analogous to pulling weeds—you've got to pull the roots out too. Get to the core of the judgment you're having, erring on the side of danger. Say it in full no matter how crazy or specific or random it might sound. Anything less will often result in the judgment persisting. (Again, this applies to willing participants, people who have agreed beforehand.)

Sharing judgments is a way of not taking them too seriously. I'll say that again: sharing judgments, expressing them out loud, is a way of not taking them so seriously. In my experience the judgments are so surface level, but you don't realize how surface level they are until you share them, because only then is the obstacle removed, which allows you to see things about that other person that you couldn't see before. You start to learn about him or her (and yourself) in a way you couldn't when you were still locked up in your head listening to your own stories. I don't believe I'm too far off when I say that almost every time I facilitate this exercise, those who had judgments end up more connected and more curious about the people they were judging, and those who were judged end up more liberated in who they are, regardless of others' opinions.

***

This exercise can also be done with resentments. Everything else would stay the same, but instead of sharing a judgment about someone else, you share a resentment. You would say, for example, "Timothy, I resent *you* for interrupting me." A lot of times I hear people sharing resentments like this: "I resent that interruption." Notice how it's not directed at a specific person, because the normal conditioning promotes indirect communication. To break that norm, we want to be direct, and speak directly to the person we have a resentment towards. That means looking them in the eye, saying his or her name, and saying "I resent YOU for..." Sharing resentments is a way of sharing love, maybe the most neglected way in this day and age. The reason we share resentments is that they get in the way of another form of love: appreciation. Another reason we share them is to get them out of the way, which allows us to share another form of love: *appreciation.*

***

Not all judgments are bad. A good judgment can be known as an appreciation. As a group, we get up and mingle once more, and this time the goal is to take a moment to look each person in the eye, tell them one thing that we appreciate about him or her, and give that person a hug before moving on to the next.

Similar to sharing our negative judgments, sharing our appreciations directly and openly rather than subtly or in code was an under-developed practice of expressing our love. In the past, we might have felt shy about complimenting another person for a specific quality or trait. We might have told ourselves a story about why we shouldn't express that appreciation. "Maybe she'll think I'm hitting on her." "Maybe he'll think I'm jealous or envious." "Maybe he'll think I'm gay." Those are fun stories, and they can be even more fun (funcomfortable) by being shared.

So, as you go around the room, you'll lock eyes with someone, and that means it's their turn. Go up to him or her and say, "I appreciate you for calling me up on my story earlier. The way you did it wasn't at all shutting me down. I actually felt like you were holding the space for me to express something deeper."

The same guideline applies with appreciations as does with resentment. "I appreciate YOU ..." A lot of people have the habit of saying "I appreciate it" or "I appreciate that" which is still a form of being less direct.

"Jordan, I appreciate you for making us breakfast. There was a lot of love in it and I felt very grateful eating it."

"Amy, I appreciate you for talking about your son in the last exercise. Hearing you speak about your role as a mom made me think about my own mom, and I imagine that I saw her through you in a very unique way."

"Timothy, I appreciate you for your handstand practice. It inspires me to be more systematic with my own physical potential."

I imagine that after reading this exercise you might think it's pretty simple, so simple in fact that maybe you're "smart" enough to get the gist of it without doing it. I imagine you would be missing out on one of the best exercises in the book. When you're presented with another soul in a human suit, when you're looking in their eyes and they're right in front of you, you will find yourself reaching deeper into your own heart to pull up something of value for them. You will appreciate them for things that you want to appreciate yourself for, or things you already recognize as within your capacity. You will appreciate them for things that you recognize as beyond you, or outside of your domain, and in sharing that appreciation, you'll realize that's great. Or you might be surprised to realize that the thing you appreciate about someone else is within you too, though perhaps in a unique form. Appreciating someone else's intelligence, for example, doesn't discredit your own. So and so may be an amazing athlete, which you don't consider yourself to be, but that doesn't take away anything from your own gifts. It adds to them. It adds to everything. By learning to recognize people's strengths and beauty, and expressing your appreciation for them, the world becomes more obviously miraculous.

This one is more of an at-home exercise: *Record your gossip*.

Have you ever walked away from a conversation with a friend, coworker, sibling or boss and wondered how truthful that person was being? Do you catch yourself doubting how honest other people are with you? Was that the truth, the whole truth, or did they sugar coat it? Did they outright lie?

I have found that the more I practice telling the truth in my day to day life, the less those kinds of questions arise, and that's because the more I tell the truth, the more I know what the truth sounds and feels like, and the better I can detect when people aren't being forthcoming. When people don't tell me the truth, or when I imagine that they are being deceptive, I, practicing honesty, ask them about it, I call them up, I don't walk away with the feeling of incompleteness, and I let go of assumptions.

To that end, here is an exercise that you can do at home starting immediately: Record Your Gossip. By "gossip" I mean anything you might say *about* someone to someone else, but which you would be afraid or nervous to say directly to him or her.

Here's how it works: the next time you catch yourself talking to someone about someone else, pull out your phone (which it seems most people always have handy) and press the record button. You might be talking to your friend about another friend, or to your dad about your mom, or to your mom about your spouse's mom, etc. When you notice that you're talking about someone, that's the "check engine light" going off, that's your awareness being dialed up. Heed that alarm by pressing record and holding yourself accountable.

Feel that? That's the filter of your heart springing into action. That's your heart flexing to get it right. Whatever it is you wanted to say or were saying about the other person, the presence of a microphone causes the lesser, gossipy parts of you to go silent. Why? Because they've been caught in the act. I imagine you will feel more conscious about what you're saying, and you will begin to speak in a way that is more truthful and holistic, rather than deflecting by projecting your pain onto an innocent bystander or someone who is not in your presence. You might ask yourself, why am I talking about this person? What does that part of me want to achieve by talking about this other person? Do I really want those things to be true for him or her?

When you're done gossiping, listen to the recording. Listen to what you said. Do you still stand by it? Did it contribute to the creation of a better world? Do you feel better or worse having said it? I believe one of the fastest ways to figure out what we think about ourselves is to hear what we say about other people. In that case, what does your gossip say about you?

I would compare gossip to polluted or chemical-laden tap water. It seems to be full of invisible motives and intentions, projections, toxic soul-seepage—all of which can be cleansed and filtered by the presence of a microphone—which brings light to the situation, catalyzing your higher self, which catalyzes getting your intention right. You'll notice when your intention is incongruent. You might trip over your words, and struggle to put sentences together. What made sense internally will make less sense spoken aloud, especially when you factor that the person you're talking about might eventually hear what you say. Gossip is an indication that at that moment you may lack integrity. Presumably you lacked integrity in the past too, because the urge to gossip might be an indication that you didn't speak up in the past, that is, to the person you're now gossiping about. Gossip is a way of leaking energy. It can be draining. It's a reflection of other ways you might be leaking energy and not tapped into your fullest potential. If you have the time to talk or complain about someone else, you also have the time to talk to that person. That way, rather than complaining about a situation that you aren't doing anything to mend, you take an active role in co-creating a better outcome.

Another thing about gossip is that it's similar to playing God. People who gossip are talking about others in a way they probably think is truthful, but then they are withholding that truth from the other person because they think he or she can't handle it. They think that what they are saying might impact him or her in some way, so they deprive that person of the information. They assume they know what is best for someone else. How do they really know I imagine most people want to hear the truth, even if (especially if) that truth might be elevating or controversial.

So, after you've listened to the recording, confess to the person you were gossiping about the next time you see them. Say something like, "Mom" (or Dad or Joe or Jessica or whomever), "the other day after we saw each other I wasn't happy with the encounter, and I ended up talking about you to someone else after the fact. I even recorded it, so you can listen if you want. But better than that, I'd like to talk to you a little more if you're interested."

Recording my gossip definitely made my heart speed up a little. It hugs the line between honesty and taboo. A few times I actually sent the recording to the person I was gossiping about as soon as I had made it. I don't recommend that for everyone or for every situation, but I was surprised at how favorably people reacted. Where I might have feared some heated discussion, the result was usually genuine interest and care. People took me seriously. They either called me right away, or texted, or sent their own gossip about my gossip back to me. The sharing of these thoughts drew us closer together, helped instill our trust in one another, and gave us a stronger bond. It removed blockage rather than adding to the debris. The next time we met in person, we felt more cordial and good-natured, less needy and manipulative, and more mutually known and seen.

So much of gossip is about assigning blame to someone who isn't there to defend him or herself. The blame game is itself a great reminder, because if you're going to blame someone for something negative in your life, be sure to blame them for all the positive things in your life too. This realization can catalyze us letting go of the blame game entirely, and realize that it's always ourselves.

The goal in recording your gossip is ultimately to let go of resorting to gossip. When you gossip about someone, you put words between you and them. Speaking directly to them, on the other hand, using your heart as a guide, bridges that gap and brings you closer together. I often hear the excuse that "so and so can't take it if I speak honestly with him or her." I think that excuse is a story, and that story is a cover up for another story. It's not that they can't take your honesty—how would you know unless you give it a go? Rather, you don't want to do what it takes because you fear the reaction they might have to your honesty ... or the reaction you might have to your own honesty.

For that fear, I believe it is helpful to consider that maybe the people who "can't" handle your honesty, or the people who aren't really interested in your honesty, have an important role to play in your life.

Talk *to* people the way you would talk *about* them to your best friends. The more I'm able to do that, the more I find that most people seem to become better friends.

Awareness is the volume button
of consciousness.

Chapter 9

Not Everyone Who
Craps On You...

A family of birds was flying south one winter, when one of the birds got tired and lagged behind. The other birds encouraged it and cheered it on, but it was too exhausted and too far back to follow. As the flock went on the bird sank lower in the sky. It saw a field, drifted down, and landed.

With the family gone, the bird felt alone. As time passed the wind got colder, and the colder it got the less the bird moved, the more it curled itself up tight.

Some grazing cows came passing by and started eating close beside it. One of the cows, maybe on purpose, maybe not, pooped on the bird—literally pooped right on top of it, a huge pile that covered the bird completely.

The bird was shocked at first, indignant, grossed out. How dare you, the bird thought. Get that crap out of here.

But then again, the poop was warm. Really warm. It wrapped the bird up and gave protection from the wind. The bird liked stewing in it. It felt good to be out of the wind, so good in fact that the bird slowly uncurled itself. It began to move, which made it even warmer. Soon it felt warm enough and energized enough to fly.

The bird started to wriggle and climb its way out. It reached the surface, however, to find that the outer layer of crap had stiffened into a hard crust. The bird kicked and pecked and clawed and eventually broke through. It began to caw and cry as if for help.

Eventually the bird heard a tapping or scratching on the outside, and knew that someone had heard its cry and come to the rescue. The bird looked up, saw a hole in the crust, and the sunlight coming through. It spread its wings and flexed its legs and leaped into the air and—

Was snatched from the pile and devoured whole. Its rescuer, turns out, was actually a cat.

That's the story of the bird. *Not everyone who craps on you is an enemy. Not everyone who pulls you out of it is a friend.* Cows are cows, cats cats, and birds birds. At some point in our lives we've probably all acted like one or all three. We might have even switched roles in relation to others, playing different parts with different people. We might have alternated between cow and cat towards the same person. Maybe in the past we've benefited from being crapped on. Maybe we secretly liked it. Maybe in hindsight there were times when we didn't want to be rescued, when we wanted to stay in the crap until it became fertilizer.

There are a lot of ways to interpret this story. For me it highlights the idea that we never really know. I've had the experience (as I imagine you have too) of waking up to the realization that in relation to someone else I was acting like a cat or cow or bird, so to speak. The flip side (I've noticed this too) is that sometimes the cows, the haters, the ones who sling crap at me, turn out to be blessings. Sometimes they turn into fans, which makes me think that they are fans all along, only they haven't yet admitted it consciously yet. Their crap can be fertilizing. It can provide an interesting, even energizing contrast, that catalyzes new seeds within me to grow. Their crap, I realize, has less to do with me than it has to do with them—maybe they'll come around, maybe not.

This not knowing goes beyond relationships. I find that the more I think about things, the less I actually know, because the more I think about things, the more perspectives I can come up with, the more questions I can ask, and the more the truth of any one statement seems to depend on a lot of other variables staying the same.

I've changed my mind in the past. I've believed something one moment, strongly believed it, to the point that I might have argued with other people in defense of that belief, only to take it back later in the face of new evidence. Because that has happened to me once, I imagine it can happen two times, three times, and so on. "Knowing" what I now "know," I can trust that the things I think I "know" might change in the future.

Or, to take assumptions out of it, I don't imagine myself to know everything, and because I don't know everything, how can I be one hundred percent sure about anything? There could be things out there, in the realm of the unknown that, once they are known, will displace or recontextualize what I now know. To put it in a positive light: Every day I learn something new.

What's more important to me than finding answers is being at peace with the questions, because the questions are a symptom of learning.

I bring up this "not knowing" in the context of relationships because to me it's fundamental. As much as looking into nature reveals an inherent mystery, looking at another person, staring into their eyes and contemplating their existence is even more of a mystery. We meet each other as mutual mysteries, and what we desire is intimacy. Intimacy happens when we can be fully known and accepted for what we really are.

That's where the prayer at the end of the Self-Acceptance chapter comes in. It serves as a mantra for this chapter. *I do my thing, and you do your thing. I am not in this world to live up to your expectations, and you are not in this world to live up to mine. You are you, and I am I. If by chance we find each other, it is beautiful, but if not, it can't be helped.*

The prayer signals, on the one hand, *self-acceptance*, and on the other, *acceptance of other selves*. Every person you meet, every person you don't meet, is not merely a "you," an object, or other. Every person is an "I," who comes from somewhere and is going somewhere, just like you yourself are an "I" in constant growth and change. To me, you are you. To I, you are I. The paradox is that I am a you and you are an I. I am you, you are I. Bob Marley started his concerts not by greeting all the "yous," but by greeting each "I and I and I."

The prayer keeps it simple. It works because in our hearts we recognize it as true. I do me and you do you. We aren't here to please each other. We aren't here to worship our opinions of one another. So, don't worry about what I want and I won't worry about what you want, meaning we won't get all twisted up and bent out of shape trying to figure out how to one up the other and win some sort of victory or approval. I don't need your validation in order to be who I am, nor do you need mine. I don't need you to believe the same things that I believe. I don't need you to live your life in a certain way to make me more confident in my own. For these reasons, I'm open to being honest with you, open to being seen by you. Maybe at this moment I'm a bird that got a little tired, and maybe you're a cow or maybe you're a cat. Maybe we're none of those things, or maybe we're a combination of everything out in the pasture and beyond, who knows?

The burden we carried in the past was being highly self-conscious but deeply unaware. Freedom is a perception that we act upon. Let's let the story go of who we think we are, because maybe, just maybe, since we don't know everything, the exact opposite one is also true.

I think we're ready for this kind of honesty and transparency. After the exercises in the beginning of the book, we're more aware of our own shadows, which allows us to accept the shadows of others, so that together, we bring ourselves to light.

Here is one of the most powerful things I can say about this kind of honesty and transparency: it gets you out of the relationships that don't serve you faster, and keeps you in relationships that do serve you longer.

Choose yourself. Encourage others to choose their Self. Then you meet as kings, queens and superheroes. The degree to which you can accept and love yourself as you really are is indicative of the degree to which you can accept and love others as they really are. That, to me, is the foundation of a REALationship.

I do my thing, and you do yours. If by chance we find each other, it is beautiful. If not, we'll try to help it. Either way, it's beautiful.

You have all the time you want.

Chapter 10

There Is No Waste of Time

W hat is a retreat? It is a verb, and a noun. It is the act of retiring or withdrawing from something that is dangerous or disagreeable, and it is the place to which one retires, a place of privacy or safety. It is the movement of an army when it surrenders a held position, and it is the new location to which that army goes in order to assess and regroup. After that assessment, one might go right back into the same fray, or one might change directions altogether. One might decide that the division of "retreat" from "real life" is artificial, and choose to live in a new way. A caterpillar retreats into its cocoon, perhaps thinking that this is the end. That retreat evolves its life entirely and this is its new beginning.

One of the aims of this experience is to step out of the rushed reality of the rat race and step into the abundance of eternal time—breaking the normalized routines that a lot of people have unconsciously followed for most of their lives, and allowing them to align with a more natural rhythm.

"What time is it?"

Now.

"What day is it?"

Today.

Don't let any clock or calendar tell you otherwise. Before the holidays were invented, every day was holy. In the eyes of the Creator, they still are. Isn't every day a birthday, and Earth Day, and Christmas, and Thanksgiving? Is there any good reason why we don't celebrate mothers, fathers, and children every day? Are there really days where it is "ok" to be less consciously grateful for the lives we have, where we can run on auto-pilot from the time we wake up to the time we go to bed because tomorrow is more important? Is there a way we can wake up to the truth of every moment?

There is, though in order to do so, we might first have to go to sleep...

Imagine going to bed not at a prescribed bedtime, but when you feel tired. Imagine giving yourself permission, in advance, to sleep as long as you desire, and to wake up when you feel well rested. Imagine that it's Friday night, or Saturday night, or whatever night of the week precedes a day in which you don't have anything on your schedule, and tell yourself that in the morning, you will wake up naturally, with no alarm clock, no ringing telephone.

Now imagine doing that not just tonight, but every night. In fact, imagine everyone on Earth doing that every night—going to bed when they're tired, and waking up when they're rested.

Maybe that brings up a story about how the idea is impossible, or delusional, or too far out. But maybe also a flutter of good feeling, a tempting "what if," a sensation of time expanding. How would you be different—mood wise, health wise, job wise, etc.—if you could reclaim your natural sleep pattern? How do you imagine other people might be different, if they could reclaim theirs? How would we treat other people, if we started treating ourselves in this way?

In the past, a lot of people used alarm clocks because they didn't trust themselves to be in certain places at certain times—they "needed" the alarm in order to stay on track. But whose track were they trying to stay on?

The alarms were an indication that those people might have been living in a false way, trying to do things that were out of alignment with who they were. They "needed" the alarm in order to get themselves to do things that they might have instinctively balked at. By imposing a wake-up time, they imposed a bed time, which imposed their evening, their afternoon, their morning. No wonder people's lives got out of balance. There was no rhythm, no flow. It was all externally dictated, obeying serpents rather than proceeding from God within. The alarm overrode their subconscious intelligence, waking them up in a false way.

***

Before going to bed tonight, try turning off your alarm, and giving yourself permission to sleep as long as you want and wake up as late as you want. The point is to wake up naturally—no alarm clocks, no ringing telephones. Whether it's 4 am, 8 am, or 12 pm, sleep when you're tired and wake up when you're rested. You might sleep all in one stretch, or you might find yourself in a polyphasic cycle.

It's interesting that this exercise, waking up naturally, which to me is pretty simple and almost common sense, can trigger so many people. Before they even try it, they give me all the reasons why they can't. "What about work, what about school, what about practice?"

What about them, I say. I'm not asking here for the story that prevents you from sleeping naturally, I'm simply asking if you'd like to, and if so, do it.

Take a day and decide the night before not to set an alarm. Tell yourself that you're going to sleep naturally and you're going to wake up naturally. There's no hurry, there's no deadline. Tell yourself it's summer, it's Saturday, it's vacation—whatever you associate with an abundance of time. You close your eyes, then, with a feeling of trust—that you have all the time you desire.

That's the feeling, I imagine, that leads to the deepest rest. That's the feeling that calls up our highest dreams. The thought of it changes our mood, our outlook, and our attention. Nothing to catch up to, nothing to fall behind. We can shift our focus from the list of things we have to do, to the list of things we want to do.

I wonder if the degree to which we can't sleep as long as we naturally want to is the degree to which we might be out of sync with our divine intelligence, meaning that the more things in our lives that we'd have to shift around or change to make this kind of sleeping possible—whether it's a job or relationship or living situation—the more stuff there is that we've allowed to block our light. That's why something as seemingly simple as getting your sleep right can lead to such big transformation, because it catalyzes you to reorganize and prioritize.

If you have to push work back an hour or so to make this happen, push it back. Do what you have to do so that you can experience going to bed and waking up unhurried.

***

One of our biggest deceptions is the story we told ourselves in the past that in order to do what we wanted to do, we had first better do what we're supposed to do. The rationalization was that by fulfilling other people's obligations before our own we served our time and thus earned the right to "self-indulge." If we didn't do things in that order, we were called "selfish" or "egotistical" or "self-centered" or "narcissistic." The challenge with that thinking, though, is that the passion we put off *this time* we also put off *next time*. And the next. New obligations sprang up. There was always, according to the story, aka the "rational lie," something else we should do first, something more immediate and less selfish.

I don't get it. To me that's like giving from an empty cup, and when that happens, as my friend Brandon Hawk says, you give beyond your capacity, and turn the receiver into a thief. How many thieves are created every day by doing things we don't want to do? How much resentment builds up, and where does that build up find release?

It seems to me that when you do what you want to do you start to feel the way you want to feel. You start to feel good. Feeling good, I think, is the sensation of your cup overflowing, and when your cup is overflowing you give freely to others, and let go the mindset of scarcity. This creates a feeling of connection—with yourself, with your environment, with your tribe. That connection gets you into a state of flow, which is a heavenly state to be in. Why wouldn't we desire to be in that state more often than not? Why wouldn't we desire for others to be in that state too?

So, after waking up (naturally) allow yourself at least a few minutes to do something you want to do, simply because you desire to do it. Daydreaming, swimming, walking, running, meditating, cooking breakfast, masturbating, making love, playing a game, even checking your Facebook, and so on. Whatever it is, do it. If thoughts of guilt come up, then thoughts of guilt come up. So what? Observe them, appreciate them, entertain them, and find out what they're telling you, what other thoughts they lead to.

Maybe the first day it's five minutes, five minutes before you turn your attention to something out of obligation. Great. The next day, make it ten minutes. The day after that, twenty. A week later, thirty. And so on. Over time—maybe a lot of time, maybe not—allow those morning moments to swell and take over more of your day as more of your divine Self wakes up. Another good indicator might be the degree of contrast between these mornings and the rest of your day. The less it feels like you're being yanked from what you want to do into something you "have" to do, the better you might be doing.

You can build these types of pockets into your day, specific stretches of time in which you consciously choose to honor yourself by doing what you feel called to do. A break at lunch, an hour after work, ten minutes before bed. Evolution comes, I think, when those various pockets swell and eventually meet each other, effectively phasing out the old stories and obligations. In those pockets of time you go to the places, do the things, think the thoughts, and sing the songs that fill you up, that allow you to hear God's voice the loudest. You almost run on autopilot, meaning you go wherever your soul (your connection to God) prompts you. That's what inspiration is, those moments when the noise of the world drops off and you hear straight to the source. The more seriously you take what you hear when you're in that state, the more you choose to build your life around those things, the more you honor yourself and your God. You start to choose to spend your time, your attention and intention on things that you consider to be the highest.

That's how you get in the flow. Even if no two days are the same, they all have that rhythm and momentum which comes from honoring your highest Self. Being in flow is like dreaming wide awake. You're both more there and less there. Something deeper has taken the reins. Your inner avatar comes on. That avatar is your most authentic Self, the reason you were born you, and not someone else. There is something about you, when you're in your highest state, that is different from everyone else on Earth. That thing is closely connected to your gift, which is the contribution you can give to others. Inspiration is what turns the avatar on. It's not to the exclusion of things like logic or work or exertion. It's what gives birth to them, and shows you the things you want to work at and exert yourself for. Your best work happens when you feel best. Make your "work" be something that allows you to feel good and God. That's probably the most sustainable "job" you can have.

*Life is a choice; the meaning is
what you make it.*

Chapter 11

Everything Is Natural

I believe that everything on Earth, everything around and within you, is natural. Everything you can see, touch, taste, smell, or hear, all inner space and outer space.

There's no such thing as "all natural" or "not natural," because everything is. We are made of the same materials as the Earth, and the Earth is made of the same materials as the universe, and the universe is made of the same materials as the multiverse, and on and on. There is nothing outside our world, no shelf labeled "unnatural" from which we can grab a bottle of something and sprinkle it onto an otherwise natural dish and thereby make it unnatural.

Even high fructose corn syrup is natural. Even GMOs. Both are the result of a human being (which is a natural being) interacting with other natural beings, to isolate parts of that being and enhance certain characteristics—sweetness, in the case of high fructose corn syrup.

This chapter is about diet and physical well-being, though my intention is to use diet to open up the consideration that the food we eat, and the way we eat it, influences other aspects of our lives, because how we do anything is indicative of how we do everything. We are what we eat, but maybe it is equally true that we are what we look at, what we listen to, what we touch, taste and think.

The poison is in the dosage and the medicine is in the poison. It is possible to have too much of a "good" thing, and it is possible to have too little of a "bad" one. It is also possible to cleanse your health away, just as it is possible to eat yourself to death. I'll never forget what our taxi driver in Jamaica told us as he escorted us around the island in search of the best coconuts. He sagely expressed, "Be careful what you eat or you'll dig a grave with your teeth."

My grandma lived to be 100. She was one of the "healthiest" people I knew, and yet, as far as I could tell, she didn't follow a strict dietary regimen, or ride some roller coaster of splurging and purging, or gluttony and fasting. She didn't feel guilty about eating dessert, and she didn't eat her vegetables simply because she was supposed to. She ate when she was hungry, and stopped eating before she felt full. In her later years, when her caloric demands were low, she could seemingly make a meal out of a single strawberry, by savoring it, by eating it slowly, and by being grateful and present as she did.

I take my inspiration from her, though my own journey has gone down many paths. Sometimes, the path I found myself on became the path I lost myself on.

It starts in the house I grew up in, where I was on a strict "see food" diet. Meat, potatoes, vegetables, Oreos, Coca Cola, Fruit Loops, Scooby Snacks, you name it. If I saw it, I ate it. At school the lunch often included chicken nuggets shaped like dinosaurs. I even drank Coca Cola as my sports drink when I was captain of the high school baseball team. As for the milk, let's just say it was highly manipulated by humans before it even left the cow.

"It's just food." That pretty much sums up my attitude at the time. The "see food" diet continued through my childhood and into high school. The difference was that now I wanted to gain weight so that I could throw a faster fastball. I started eating more—more meat, more fast food, more whatever, while also supplementing creatine and protein. It worked in the sense that I got bigger and stronger, though to judge from photos, I was also puffy and inflamed.

When I got to college my priorities shifted from sport performance to aesthetics. Girls didn't care how fast I could throw a baseball, only how fast it looked like I could throw one (or at least that's what I thought at the time). My workouts at this time had more to do with getting muscular than with being healthy and mobile.

I still ate a lot of meat and protein, but thanks to inspiration from my brother, who had recently gotten ripped, I also chowed down on green vegetables with dinner. That one change made a noticeable difference.

The climax of this *seefood* approach came the year I graduated college, at a New Year's Eve party I put on. For a lot of reasons, I didn't eat much that day, and before the party all I had was an apple. I wasn't as aware of my body then as I am now, so I didn't hesitate to drink alcohol once the party got started. Nor did I hesitate to mix in a cigar and cannabis. Shortly into my own party, I was so messed up I had to leave. I asked my friends to take me to a hotel.

I'd seen people throwing up on the side of the road before, and I always wondered how they let it happen. That night, I found out. Before reaching the hotel, I hollered to pull over and emptied my stomach onto the curb. Once there, I fell immediately into bed. I actually started crying because of how miserable I felt.

I remember waking up some time later, looking around the room at my friends who by now were also messed up, and commenting to myself at how strange they looked. I went into the bathroom to puke again, but when nothing came up I stood at the sink and splashed water in my face. The room was spinning, but by looking at my own eyes, I was able to steady myself. I stared into them for a long time, seeing more layers and depth and nuance than I'd seen before. Eventually I started to pray. I pleaded with God to remove from my body whatever it was that was still making me sick. I promised to never again consume any of the things I had that night, and to stop polluting my body altogether. I would stay clean, I decided, until the next calendar landmark...which happened to be my brother's birthday in February.

It's strange...I seemed to sober up right there. I splashed more water on my face, then walked out of the bathroom and saw my friends laying around, and told them that I was going back to the party. Which I did. And had an awesome time.

The next day I realized that my brother's birthday was exactly forty days and forty nights away, and that synchronicity inspired me to up the ante. I decided to cut out even more than weed, alcohol, and tobacco. I dropped coffee, masturbation, candy, and everything else I deemed to be junk food.

His birthday came and went, and I kept going.

Here is where the appeal of diets becomes especially potent. Diets, like dogmas, are alluring in their certainty. The mantra "all or nothing" is simple. It's clean division with no remainder, and leaves little room for doubt or deliberation. Sometimes it is easier to be told what one can and cannot do than it is to make and take responsibility for one's own decisions. Whenever a question arises, all a person has to do is pull out the stone tablet somebody else wrote and read it for the answer. Adopt a diet or a dogma, and one no longer has to think for oneself.

The appeal of a raw vegan diet is that it is clean and cleansing. Its promise is to make sure there is nothing bad inside your body, and it carries the added benefit of being morally superior to other diets, especially those that include meat. At that time in my life I wanted to be clean, both inside and out, and I enjoyed the newfound energy and clarity I felt. And because my brothers and I were traveling to places like Costa Rica for retreats and surfing, the transition to pure raw vegan seemed natural.

At first it was great. My energy, like I said, shot way up, instead of dropping like I had expected. My eyes seemed clearer, my skin glowed, everything about me seemed more radiant. I was pooping, I imagined, as free and easy as a monkey for the first time in years. My brothers reported similar results. We felt clean, converted, born again. We spent the days surfing in the sunshine and eating starfruit on the shore—in addition to coconuts, mangos, papayas, star apples, milk fruit, chermoya, and jackfruit. The challenges arose when it came time to go back home to Georgia, and the amount of fresh tropical fruits became limited. We had discovered the gospel, and the last thing we wanted to do was lose it. So, we made sure that didn't happen. Our business was mostly travel anyway, first as mobile marketers and tour managers, and later as retreat hosts, so we made sure to travel to places and host retreats where our food, literally, was everywhere: islands, tropical locations, California. Transit presented some challenges, as the airports were like food deserts littered with kryptonite. We began packing less clothes to have more room for fruit.

I was surprised, overall, that it wasn't harder. On the one hand, the menu of permissible food was limited, but on the other hand, there was no shortage. For months I felt amazing, and experienced a newfound appreciation for nature that I might never have known had I not gone off meat and cooked foods.

The Earth, I realized, provides everything. Not that anything I ate before that point came from anywhere other than the Earth (because it's all natural), but it usually came from the Earth via the hand and obvious MANipulation of someone else. The feeling of picking produce straight from the tree or vine on which it grew, however, and immediately eating it, was empowering and eye-opening. In that pure and simple act the fingerprint of man's manipulation was almost hidden from sight. In addition, it brought clarity and understanding into the natural seasons and cycles of ripeness and life in general.

Those cycles carried over and were reflected in the seasons of my own life. Overall, I felt clean and unadulterated, like I was getting back to something primal and elemental—the bodily equivalent of unlearning all the things I'd been forced to learn. I also noticed that I was less aggressive, less combative. I was more willing to glow with the flow. I grew my hair out, took fewer showers, let go of deodorant and soap and strangely enough, felt cleaner and smelled better.

But the purity that makes raw veganism so alluring is also what makes it so punishing. Purity is an ideal, an abstraction dangling above a distant horizon. The closer you get, the further away it seems. In pursuit of this ideal, slowly but surely, my life began to revolve around food. I began noticing sensations that I imagined were symptoms of anxiety—all in relation to my food choices and options. If I didn't have a bundle of spotted bananas nearby (aka "dinosaur wieners"), the nervousness was almost palpable. Eating is one of the most social activities humans engage in, and yet, I couldn't go out or to a friend's house without thinking about what I was going to eat. Non-organic produce presented a quandary. The sight of someone eating meat created a flashing sensation that I associated with anger.

I had heard stories from fellow raw vegans about cravings and hunger. Confessions, really. Some of them reported shame about having cheated on their diets by gorging on meat in secret, only to puke it all up later. I remember one confession that really impacted me. A young *vegan* woman had admitted to gorging on meat in her closet. Their confessions rang true to my own challenges. I too had cheated. My friends and I, in the effort of expelling all cravings for meat, had gone to a Brazilian steakhouse one night in Costa Rica to gorge ourselves. The next day I woke up in a sort of food hangover filled with shame. I felt polluted and clogged up. The only positive, as far as I could tell, was that the desire to eat meat was temporarily vanquished—the thought of it was no longer tempting, but grossed me out.

That was the start of an addiction-like cycle of using cheat meals once or twice a month. They served two purposes. First, they provided a light at the end of the tunnel, a distant reward I could look forward to and stay motivated. Second, they were a sort of punishment, making me so sick as to kill my cravings. It didn't seem healthy to me, but I rationalized that it was normal.

After a few months on this cycle, I seemed to break through. I no longer needed the cheat meals, I no longer slipped up, and for the next six months I ate nothing but raw, organic, and vegan.

The symptoms were subtle at first, but visible. My gums receded. My hair thinned. My skinned seemed to dull. I got skinnier and fatter at the same time. My parents and acquaintances began to look at me strangely, because part of my rawness was letting my hair grow even more and neglecting or looking down on personal hygiene. Some of their comments shook my dogma, caused me to doubt, but I made sure not to show it. Outwardly I became even stricter in my diet and more adamant in my faith. They just don't know any better, I told myself. (The lesson here is that arguing with someone against a behavior that you think is bad for them might be the least effective way to get them to change that behavior, because it incites more resistance. When you provide someone with all the reasons why they "shouldn't" do something or eat something, they automatically begin to construct the opposing case.)

Inside I was questioning, and I was seeing signs I couldn't ignore. For example: the anger and wrath that fellow believers directed towards heretics, shoulding and shaming everyone who believed differently. That shoulding and shaming was also directed inwardly, and at sinners within the group. Even more puzzling was the lack of interest I now had in the opposite sex.

At a summer fruit festival, a sort of Woodstock for vegans full of young and beautiful women, I was surprised at how little interest I had in pursuing intimacy with them. Other men didn't seem as interested as I would expect. It was like a spring break without the sexual energy, because all the energy was directed towards our food.

People were falling in love, not necessarily with each other, but with certain fruits and vegetables. Some compared mangoes and bananas, or bragged about who had brought the most exotic fruit to the party. People tried durian or jackfruit for the first time and were converted, while any support of meat or animal products was taboo.

I might have gotten over these observations were it not for the observation that I no longer woke up with something I'd heard was normal for young men, *morning wood*. I hadn't had that in months.

One day my brother took a bite of salmon, and I freaked out on him. I exhibited the same kind of anger towards him that I'd observed in others. He called me out on it and told me to look in the mirror.

I realized that my anger might have been hiding the fact that I secretly wanted a bite too. I decided to listen to myself (and to my dad, who was encouraging me to give it a try) by taking a bite. The next morning, that thing that hadn't happened in months spontaneously happened. My boxer shorts were like a tepee, held up from within by an old friend.

That's when I knew my diet was over. I later got my testosterone checked, and it turned out that my hormonal chart read like that of an eighty-year-old man.

The Buddhists have a metaphor about using a boat to cross the river, and then dropping the boat once you get to the other side. The tendency some people have is to continue carrying the boat when they no longer need it, so that it eventually slows them down. That hormone test, as well as the evidence in my pants (or lack thereof) and the advice I got from other guys, convinced me to drop it.

* * *

That was five years ago. My diet now changes from day to day based on where I am and what I'm doing. I trust that the way to nourish myself is not by adopting someone else's dogma, and not by creating my own, but by observing certain parameters and guidelines based on my own experience. The attachment to getting answers from somewhere outside myself may have been part of the sickness I was originally overcoming.

I've learned that there is a difference between eating to survive, eating to cope, and eating to thrive. I've learned to let go of perfection, and that what matters is what I do most of the time, or out of habit. I've learned that quick-fixes are usually short-lived and not sustainable in the long term, and I've learned that different people can eat the exact same food and get different results. I've learned that food is fuel for my fire, not the fire itself. My spirit is the fire, and that fire can burn, clean, and refine almost anything, if my intention is right.

Getting to this point involved learning to be ok with the sensation of hunger, and allowing myself to actually feel it before making it go away with food. Hunger is a primal sensation, and the way we deal with it might be indicative of how we deal with other sensations. I wonder if that is why so many religious and spiritual practices incorporate rituals of fasting, abstaining from taking nourishment. Whether it's going days at a time without food, not eating until the sun goes down, or merely skipping breakfast, there seems to be physical and spiritual benefits to experiencing hunger. Spiritually, I imagine that people go to the desert and abstain from food for a time when they are wanting clarity on some challenge or aspect of their life.

When someone is in that position, food might be a distraction, something that keeps them from getting to the core of whatever issue they're working through. Instead of sitting with the emotion or sensation, they might eat impulsively as a mild form of self-sabotage. They might eat something, not feel satisfied, eat more, not feel satisfied, and eat more still. In those instances, no amount of food will satisfy, because it's not food they are hungry for, and the answer to that challenge is not in the fridge or pantry.

Some holistic practitioners talk about how fasting gives the body the opportunity to cleanse itself and regenerate, while others say skipping breakfast allows them to focus on other tasks and be more productive during the day.

Additionally, many modern dehydrated people have mistaken thirst for hunger.

I doubt anyone would think it strange to say that drinking wine instead of tequila might influence the kind of night one is going to have, or even more drastically, drinking only water. One would expect that to be the case, which is why over the years we've experimented so much with different spirits. It is the same with food. Eating meat produces different energetic results in your body than eating plants. Eating sugar does something different than eating fat, and eating the two combined does something different still.

I've noticed that a lot of people seem to eat foods that don't agree with them, and then mask the symptoms of that disagreement, because they're either moving too quickly or too distractedly to appreciate and make choices based on the feedback. "It's just food," they say and try to get it as cheaply as possible. Pharmacies help perpetuate this cycle, because anyone can buy a pill to suppress almost any symptom, from heartburn to indigestion to headaches to runny noses to acne. Solely relying on these cover ups is the dietary equivalent of damming one's emotions, which often results in more severe damning.

This is why I'm not on the *seefood* diet anymore, nor am I on a restrictive vegan or paleo diet. Some days I eat meat, some days I eat pancakes, some days I eat salad. Some days I eat breakfast, some days I don't eat anything at all, or at least not until dinner. My "diet" is simple: I don't eat anything I don't believe is good for me, and before putting anything in my mouth, I choose to believe that it is healthy. ("Oh, so I can just sit around eating candy all day, but as long as I tell myself that it's good for me I'll be ok?" Well, it depends on whether you truly believe it, and at this point in the book, having done the prior exercises and gotten in touch with your inner responses, I imagine you will sense whether you truly do or not. From my perspective, that question, the way it is worded, seems more deflective than sincere.

Whenever I go to a restaurant, they give me a menu. For the most part I can only order things directly on that menu. In the same way, I believe that wherever I am living, wherever I have chosen to live, God has provided a menu for that location. And even though everything is natural, I believe that if I want to be in optimal health and divine brilliance, it is in my best interest to eat what is directly around me—the plants that grow best in that climate and the animals that thrive there. I figure I might as well shop locally too, to support the people and businesses around me. Whatever I'm going to eat, I make the best of it. I remind myself to be grateful and appreciative for what I am able to consume. If I don't believe it is good for me, I either change my beliefs or I don't eat. In this way food gives me the chance to check in with myself to see how I am feeling, and to decide based on that rather than on the opinions of someone else.

A good practice is to pray before eating, as so many traditional societies have done and still do. It connects us to our food and prepares the body and spirit to receive it. I like to take a moment to pray and reflect on all that went into the food that I'm about to eat.

That means the ingredients. It means the animals and what they ate. It means the sun and the rain and the cycle of the seasons. It means the farmers who cultivated the land, the people who made and operated the machinery. It means for the truck drivers, the pilots, the railroad workers, the engineers, the chefs and the dishwashers. On and on and on. You'll find, I imagine, that it is harder to feel disconnected from the world when you practice gratitude for everything you eat. Each morsel is a chain of connections leading back to the environment from which we came. By eating it, you too are forming a link in that chain.

In praying for every thing, you pray for Everything, because that's how much it takes to make a meal possible.

Everyone is telling the truth...
about themselves.

Chapter 12

Speaking In Prayer

If there is one thing we own, I might say it is our voice. Why speak if we don't want to be heard? Every word we say, even if it is silent and to ourselves, is heard by the Creator—and how do we know that the Creator doesn't hear it as a prayer?

The more I travel around, the more people I meet, the more I keep realizing the same thing: everyone is telling the truth...about themselves. The challenge, I find, is that I'm not sure a) if they believe it, and b) if the truth they're telling is the one they want to tell, that is, the truth they want to be true for their lives. Even if they're talking about someone or something else, they're still revealing some sort of truth about themselves. (And in the case of lying, sometimes they're the mostrevealing).

Like most realizations that seem to strike out of the blue, this one, in hindsight, must have been something I'd already been thinking for some time. It was towards the end of a retreat and I was listening to a woman—let's call her Anne—talk about her life back home, the things she was and wasn't going to do differently from now on. She had a large and what I imagined to be cumbersome suitcase on the ground beside her. I hadn't seen that suitcase since the first day when she arrived at the airport wheeling it along behind her. Of course, everyone brought some baggage with them, but this woman, judging by the size of the suitcase, had packed for two weeks instead of four days. The first thing we did was take it to the retreat house and stow it—out of sight and mind. After that, we were free as a group to go out, free to hike, explore, polar plunge, and for a brief time let ourselves be known.

Anne had done all that, had consistently gone outside her comfort zone. It was the last day now, the last hour in fact, and the suitcase, everything she had brought with her, was back at her side ready to go home.

"I'm so grateful for this experience," she said, "and I know I've learned a lot. I think you all are incredible people and I'm happy I got to know you and I'd love to stay in touch."

Slowly, the "real world" crept back into her speech.

I really hope I can incorporate some of what I've learned when I get back home. I don't want to lose this feeling I have right now. I feel light, both in the sense of not heavy and in the sense of having my dark spots lit up. I'm afraid I'm going to lose it. It's going to be hard, because when I'm home..."

It's no mistake that the quote drifts off, because that's when I stopped hearing her actual words, though I can guess which ones she used: my job, bills, I can't, I have to, I have a family, 'why, because' and but (a lot of buts). It was almost like I could see the spark go out of her, as a cloud of the "real world" passed before her eye. A minute ago, her vision was open and unobstructed, now it narrowed to focus on the obstacles. I could hear her subconscious speak through every word she said, as though she was giving herself away, revealing her secret motives. It was more confessional than an actual confession, only she didn't know it. She didn't necessarily believe what she was saying, but she wasn't awake enough at that moment to question it. Her subconscious, her inner saboteur, what Napoleon Hill might call the devil, was subtle, similar to her actual voice; it slipped into her speech undetected.

In short, that feeling she said she wanted to keep, she was unwittingly preparing to lose. By convincing us of why it might happen, she was convincing herself of why it was going to happen. She subconsciously knew that if we bought her story, she could buy it too. She could privately confirm her own bias, the one she kept like a secret pact to herself: "things don't work out, I'm not meant to be happy, I'm damned, I'm not born lucky, this is the way it has to be." By repeating her rationalizations aloud, in the present tense, she was projecting them outward, casting them onto the canvas of her reality.

There was a part of me that could empathize, that *wanted* to empathize, that wanted to say yes, it is hard, it's very hard. There was another part of me, however, that wanted to say no, it's really not. You might call the first part of me my human side, and the second part some other side, but even that division, which is how I thought of it in the past, is a story. It's not a matter of what I "should" do any more than it's a matter of what she "should" do. It's a matter of how do I serve her best, and to me it's not by enabling her to argue for her limitations, aiding and abetting her sense of powerlessness. It's not by nodding my head and giving her the false impression that I agree that she's a victim, and that the challenges she's named are actual reasons why she can't do what she wants to do, why she can't live in accordance with her higher self.

I didn't nod. I listened. By listening to her I allowed her to listen to herself. It all made sense in her own head, but put another person there and suddenly she heard it from a different angle. The "truth" she was professing became merely a version of the truth, which is to say, a story. That story was the only thing standing between her and the life she wanted.

* * *

Early exercises, with their focus on pulling back the layers and coming clean, were about *speaking in tongue*—letting whatever comes up come out. In religious terms, it means speaking under the spell of inspiration, where the spirit overcomes a person, their eyes roll back, and they let themselves become a vessel for whatever energies come up. Oftentimes what comes up is unintelligible through language—not words, but sounds and gestures. We use those exercises as a way of tapping our inner spring and getting to the source, which involves clearing the mud away in the form of internalized stories. Get those out (out of the way) so that you can get to the real stuff underneath.

Speaking in prayer is less an exercise and more a practice. After one has tapped the source, felt and heard the difference, one realizes how much language can influence one's reality. These are abstract concepts that are challenging to explain directly instead of metaphorically, but I trust that if you've done the earlier exercises you have an idea of what I'm talking about, that is, you're familiar with feelings that seem beyond words.

I've heard that prayer is when you're speaking to God, and meditation is when you're listening to God. In prayer we put our thoughts, hearts, desires and fears out into the universe so that the higher power can listen and bear witness. In meditation we listen, as though we've shouted into a canyon and wait for the echo to come back.

My question is, in the eyes and ears of God, aren't we always praying? If the Creator hears all—does it really matter whether we shout or whisper, whether we interlock our hands, whether we say something aloud or merely think it to ourselves? If God can detect even the tiniest of things, maybe the thought that our prayers are not answered actually reveals a darker wish?

"The Word Becomes Flesh." Repeat that like a mantra. Say it again until it makes sense—not necessarily logical sense, but heart sense, soul sense, until it catalyzes the creative being inside you to say *aha* ... or *aho*. Hear yourself speak, watch yourself act, observe yourself think. The Word Becomes Flesh means that the things we say have the power to shape our reality—and not only the things we say aloud, but also the things we think, the things we say silently to ourselves.

How would you speak if you knew that everything you said would be heard as a prayer?

How would you think if you knew that your thoughts expressed your wishes?

This idea springs from the questions and realizations above. Speak in a way that you want to be taken at your word. Speak in the manner in which you want to be heard. Speak as you would if you were standing in a courtroom under oath of the highest authority.

Here's what that means specifically:

Anything you don't want in your life, speak about it in the past tense. Even if it was five minutes ago, five seconds ago, even if you are still feeling the undesirable feeling the moment you open your mouth to speak—put it in the past. Technically it is the past, because as soon as you say it, it's over, the moment has passed. Conversely, the things you do want in your life, speak about them in the present.

To go back to Anne, after she caught herself in a story, she repeated what she had said, but put it all in the past tense. She said, "In the past, it was hard for me to express myself to my family because I allowed myself to worry that they wouldn't understand what I meant. I allowed myself to worry that they would think I was crazy or weird. I even allowed myself to imagine that their judgment of me came from their own fear that I was leaving them behind, so that ultimately I felt sorry for them and held my tongue."

Do you hear the difference between that and something like, "I can't express myself because they won't understand"? Or "I can't go polar plunging in the morning or hiking in the afternoon because I have to work"?

Putting it in the present tense shirks responsibility for decisions you yourself are making. Maybe in the past, you couldn't go hiking because you had to work, which is to say, because you chose to work because you valued the security you got in health insurance and steady paychecks more than you valued the actual health and abundance you would have gotten from hiking.

That's a totally different story, with totally different implications. One is the language of power, the other the language of poverty. One is the language of responsibility, which leads to acceptance, which leads to action. The other is the language of blame, which can lead to despair and inaction. For Anne, speaking about the challenges she faced in the past immediately raises the question of what can she do about it in the present.

"Before this retreat, I had a hard time expressing myself to my family because I imagined they didn't understand me. Now I see what it really was: in the past, *I couldn't handle* the way they understood me, the way they reacted to me, and this led to some anger on my part. Now, I am more aware of this tendency, and instead of shutting down, I can be more patient with myself and with them in my self-expression. If I observe feelings of anger come up in me, I can let them know about it, rather than do what I did in the past, which was to channel it in the form of *scarasm*."

"In the past I allowed my employment to limit my options. I allowed my job to dictate what I could and couldn't do."

And now?

"Now I know that's not necessarily the case. Now, rather than discredit the things I want, I take them seriously. I figure out ways to do those things with the job I have, if it's possible, or if it's not, to either be ok with it or make a change, because there are infinite ways to get paid to pursue my passion. I can be creative with how I make my gifts valuable and available to other people."

When I hear people speak in this way, I hear individuals who stand apart from their surroundings, individuals with integrity, meaning they are whole, unimpaired, of sound mind and body. When I speak this way myself, I establish that inch of breathing room, that inch of choice and eternity between me and my circumstances.

* * *

Speaking in prayer, in addition to consciously distinguishing between past and present, is paying attention to the words you use, and letting go of the ones that no longer serve you.

Should. When you should on someone else, you imply that he or she ought to be different than he or she currently is. When you should on yourself, you do the same thing. "Shoulding" also carries the implication that you know everything, when in reality (my opinion) we don't really know anything. Everything is faith-based, and everyone is unique because everyone is on different stages of a personal journey that we often "know" very little about.

Would, Could. When you find yourself saying what you would do or what you could do, see if you can let go of talking about it and instead start doing it. Usually, "would" and "could" are followed by "but," which often leads to a story. That's why these words are "Check Engine" lights to listen closely to what you're actually saying, and if you keep using them around a certain topic, it might be a good indication to start doing that thing, or letting it go. This also applies to when you say you should have done something in the past. If you really believe you should have done it, why not see if it's too late by doing it now?

When. "I'll do this when. I'll do that when." I call that kind of talk "whening." It's one letter away from whining, and the opposite of actually winning. There is no when, there is only now. If you catch yourself "whening," know that you are putting something off to an imagined future which may or may not come.

Just. The thing about "just" is that it implies a hierarchy of importance that may or may not be there, which exists in your imagination, possibly distracting you from a shared reality with another person. This word slips into our speech (in the past) and we don't pay attention to it. "Who's there?" Just me. "What were you doing?" I was just going for a walk. Why just? Maybe you are exactly the person they're looking for, and maybe going for a walk is exactly what they want to do. "Just going for a walk" implies that maybe there's something else you think you "should" be doing, or which you imagine they think you "should" be doing, which is of potentially greater importance than going for a walk—and if that's the case, why aren't you doing it?

"Will you just cut it out with the semantics already?" Whoever asks that question imagines that cutting it out is something small and easy to do, when in reality maybe it's big, challenging, and fulfilling.

You. Have you heard people saying things like this: "When you become a parent you won't have any free time" or "When you're forty, you're over the hill" or "When you eat ice cream you gain weight"? Nowadays when someone uses the word "you" in this way, I say, "By you, do you mean you? You don't have free time? You are over the hill? You gained weight? Because you seem to be saying these things as if they're true for me, and I don't agree." I choose to honor myself enough if people project onto me, that I break normal and say what's true for *me*. Oftentimes, it seems, people use the word "you" when they mean "I."

Can't. Imagine thousands of years ago if someone said they could manipulate the rocks and sand in order to communicate with the other side of the world. They would have been considered crazy. Flash forward to the present day...what are cell phones made of? What are computers made of? Metal and glass, which is to say *Earth*. What are plastics made of? *Earth*. When I hear people say they can't do something, I think of every technological advancement in the history of the world, every new invention, every leap forward in progress. Before any of those things happened, people said they were impossible. I think of planes, trains and automobiles—not to mention all the science and innovation that comprises them. I think of athletes who overcome "career-ending" injuries, and patients who cure their ailments. So, if you notice yourself saying you can't do something, realize that if you really want to, you can, maybe not in the specific way you currently picture it, but most likely in what turns out to be an upgraded form. Instead of "I can't," give yourself the freedom to be more honest. Either you don't know how, which is a great starting place for any meaningful endeavor, or you simply don't want to.

When I hear myself say the word "can't" I stop myself right there, and reconsider what I'm about to say, because considering the abundance of evidence all around me, the word "can't" seems delusional, and maybe blasphemous. "I can't" is a story. "I can" is a greater one.

***

Now that we've shed the skin of who we no longer are by letting go of energy leaking words, it's time to imagine and incorporate the short and powerful words that do serve: I.. am...we...no...yes...you...OM. When you speak in the sacred framework of "I am" you provide a signal to the Divine that what you most desire is a done deal. In other words, you say "I am" and the Highest Power answers back ... "and so it is." When you declare "I am creative and joyful," for example, your actions and behaviors work to support your declaration. This life-affirming concept is so important for healthy individuals, families and communities. Imagine if everyone in your life adopted enough intention & attention to put the most positive "I am" statements into play (and "work" and love and contribution) and truly embodied and believed what they are saying.

***

It takes faith to speak like this, because it's not an immediate cure all. (Story?) The internal reality you achieve through your conscious use of language and your conscious reaction to thoughts might take a bit of time to come to fruition. It might happen right away, but in my experience the power of so-called positive thinking and speaking is what it does to me internally. The discipline I exercise on my own mind passes down into the rest of my being. It's a trickle-down attitude of gratitude, a mindset of growing through resistance, a lived decision to walk by faith rather than sight alone. Your physical and spiritual body is responsive to your dominating thoughts and words. It reorganizes itself according to what you tell it. When you focus on your heart's desire, your inner child conspires to make it happen. Your challenges, in other words (though this is a story), might not magically or automatically go away. What happens more often, in my experience, is that they get recontextualized. When you make the conscious decision to call stumbling blocks stepping stones, even if a moment ago you didn't believe it, a part of your mind clicks on to make that step. That's how you stretch yourself internally and *eternally* to the things you desire, by speaking about them the way you desire them to be.

By putting things in the past tense, and not allowing yourself the easy way out by using those words, you get an inch of separation from them. That inch is all that's necessary to break the programming by which one thought leads to another, which leads to an emotion, which leads to an action. Thus, speaking in prayer is also thinking in prayer, it's your conscious mind's auto-correct, which continuously calls your unconscious up.

Speaking in Prayer is different from the filtering and self-censoring we did in the past. It's not repressing what comes up, but correcting and compartmentalizing it, so as not to be carried away. If the subconscious is what drives so much of our behavior, the way to change that behavior is to reprogram the subconscious, and we can do that through language. The subconscious, the self-saboteur, the devil you get to outwit, knows it is risky to speak directly to you, but when it's triggered it will run the risk anyway. The reason it's risky is because it opens a line of direct communication with you, and makes itself vulnerable. When you "catch it in the act" you can correct it right then and there.

This is what it means metaphorically to change yourself at a cellular level. In terms of self-development, it's like aligning yourself from top to bottom, making sure all the bolts are tight and all the beams true, because every imbalance can be a leaking of energy, attention and intention.

When we are in our highest state, I believe our prayers mainly consist of gratitude. Gratitude for the life we are given.

It would almost defeat the purpose for me to inspire you into a state of gratitude by showing you what you get to be thankful for. The process of discovering for yourself what exactly you get to be grateful for is one of the benefits of the exercise. If you are a parent, or if you were God, and your children kept asking you for more—more money, more opportunities, more whatever—when they didn't appreciate what they already had, how likely would you be to give it to them?

Gratitude reciprocates and repays. Gratitude is eye-opening and transformative. I was once asked the question, *Daniel, if you're promoting gratitude as a way of getting more, how grateful, really, is that?*

If you're only grateful because you've calculated that that's the most effective means to getting more, is that really grateful? My answer is no. If you're being grateful only out of the calculated desire for more, you aren't really grateful. That is no reason, however, to not be grateful. That double-minded state is for many a stage on the way to true gratitude. Gratitude is an end in itself, which catalyzes new beginnings. If I were in such a state I would acknowledge it in my prayer.

Awareness is the volume-knob of consciousness, and recognizing that you are grateful but still desiring more is yet another level of self-acceptance.

There is no limit to self-acceptance.

I could go from the outside in, and talk about the vastness of the world you were born into, the infinite multiverse, and work my way back to the infinitesimal cells in your body. Or I could I go inside out, and talk about each of our bodies as being a single cell in the Earth, and the Earth being a single cell in an even vaster organism. The point is to find one thing to be grateful for, one single thing, and to meditate on it. What I've found is that it's hard to be grateful for one thing without being grateful for everything, because everything is connected.

It is said that Jesus turned water to wine. I wonder if that is literal or metaphorical. Did he actually transmute $H2O$ into fermented grape juice, or did he catalyze the minds of those around him into the realization that water is the stuff of life, the blood of the earth—in which case, why not call it wine? I'm not sure which miracle is more miraculous.

Objectivity is subjective.

Chapter 13

What's Working for You

I 've heard that a *tribe* is a group of people gathered around a fire telling stories to each other in order to be less afraid of what's in the dark. That idea has always resonated with me as one of the purposes of our retreats.

There is something very powerful about bringing people together and creating a space where we can explore that darkness. Seeing other people do things that they're afraid to do, watching them grow through the experience, catalyzes your own growth and expansion. I remember a man who was under the spell of thinking he was suicidal (and thinking that he had been for the majority of his life), confidently declaring by the end of the retreat, "I got me." His transformation was a gift for all of us. A woman, nearly three times my age, made sure to look me in the eyes before leaving to say, "These retreats are saving lives." I would say the retreats *change* lives, by giving people experiences and tools that they can carry with them when they leave. The exercise we often save for last—sometimes we do it at the airport before saying goodbye—is called "What's working for you, what's not working for you." We get in the circle one last time and take turns standing in the middle.

It's a gift we give each other at the end, a final look in the collective mirror that we've co-created. Even though at this point we've only been together for a short amount of time, four days, it seems as if we're old friends reunited, preparing yet again to branch out and go our separate directions. Some members of the group you might recognize as members of your long-lost tribe, while others you recognize as leaders of their own. Either way there's a connection. In four days we opened up, shared, and allowed ourselves to be seen to a degree that we might never have experienced before, therefore we know each other differently, and maybe deeper, than we know even our friends back home. We created a bond quicker and more intimately than we might have done even with our own families.

Even with that connection, the exercise is a little bit absurd. It's so subjective.

That's fine. That's actually part of the point, to acknowledge one last time the crap shoot of living up to other people's expectations. Essentially, we're sharing our judgments, and allowing the person in the middle the opportunity to observe themselves react to our judgments. Some of the judgments might ring true, some not. Someone might say something is working for you that you suspect is not working for you, and vice versa. The idea is for each person to immerse themselves in different, and oftentimes contradictory perspectives, in order to realize that at the end of the day, being yourself, being true to yourself, is the only option left.

Here's how it works. Circle up, one person in the middle, two minutes on the clock. When the time starts, the group tells the person in the middle what's not working for them—anything from their hairstyle, to their job, to their clothes, to their relationships, to their outlook, you name it. We're telling that person what we see, and not "just" physically see, but spiritually, emotionally, and energetically see considering our own imagination of past and future, our own feelings and hopes and dreams. We are seeing with as much of our whole person as we can, and reporting our observations.

So, imagining now that you are in the middle, here's what I would say is not working for you.

What's not working for you is being under the influence of suppression, limits, and rational lies.

What's not working for you is *choosing* to be under the influence of suppression.

What's not working for you is looking up to others, thinking they are better than you.

What's not working for you is looking down on others, thinking that they are worse than you.

What's not working for you is imagining that you are more spiritual than any other person...or that anything is more spiritual than anything else.

What's not working for you is desperately seeking outside approval.

What's not working for you is dogma.

What's not working for you is not wanting to upset your parents, or your in-laws, or your spouse, or your partner.

What's not working for you is a disconnect from the most motherly essence of all, Mother Nature.

What's not working for you is ignoring that call to Mother Nature, not honoring it, tiptoeing around it. By Mother Nature I also mean your inward nature.

What's not working for you is the self-deprecating laugh you do after you say something you believe is direct and powerful.

What's not working for you is the way you pretend to be more sure or less sure than you actually are.

What's not working for you is working, that is, working at a job you lack passion for, and which you yourself suspect is holding you back.

What's not working for you is reading this book for answers instead of questions.

What's not working for you is watching the news.

What's not working for you is the story you tell yourself about your weight and image.

What's not working for you is indecision.

What's not working for you is wanting to be right.

After that two minutes are up, we switch to what *is* working for that person.

So, what's working for you is your weight.

What's working for you is your health.

What's working for you are all the situations and all the people that you find to be most challenging in your life.

What's working for you are your skeptics.

What's working for you is your voice.

What's working for you is your shyness.

What's working for you is your birthmark.

What's working for you is your outgoingness.

What's working for you is your awareness that you sometimes you think you're selfish.

What's working for you is your femininity and your masculinity.

What's working for you is not knowing what you want to do.

What's working for you is working out, working in, and playing around.

What's working for you is the laugh you think is awkward.

What's working for you is your integrity, your commitment to your word.

What's working for your willingness to follow your heartbeat, especially when it leads you to the wisdom of the unknown and the unsure.

What's working for you is the time you made a joker of yourself, the time you got bullied, fired, or dumped.

What's working for you is speaking up, sharing your judgments and your disagreements.

What's working for you is asking questions.

What's working for you is answering questions (or not answering them).

What's working for you is the perception of opposites, seeing both sides of the same coin, such as jealousy and admiration, fear and excitement, faith and doubt, love and indifference.

What's working for you is listening, and seeking to listen better.

What's working for you is doing these exercises in real life (and realizing that it's always "real life")

What's working for you is practicing gratitude.

What's working for you is pursuing your inward calling.

What's working for you is imagining that you might be afraid of that calling.

In short, what's working for you is everything. The only thing that might not be working for you is your not realizing it, your pretending that it isn't the case. But then again, even that is working for you.

About the Author

Daniel Eisenman graduated Pre-Med from Emory University with a BS (Key Acronym) in Biology and even took the MCAT in 2007. Before applying to medical school to stay on the path of "NORMAL" as people advised him, he decided to "take a year off." That year off has now turned into a decade of BREAKING NORMAL while getting paid to the do the things he would pay to do, including visiting all 50 states and 20+ countries.

Daniel travels the world as a keynote speaker and facilitator of radical retreats and workshops (though he likes to call them playshops, as what's more pure than play?) based on the principles of raw honesty and emotional freedom. Daniel shows you a process of self-acceptance through self-expression by guiding you to lose your mind in order to connect to your heart while truly living inside-out.

He lives in San Diego, California with his wife, Diana, their beautiful daughter, Divina, and their amazing dog, Oriah.

APPENDIX
Top Ten Hacks for Breaking Normal

1 – WAKE UP. Wake up naturally—no alarms, no electronic devices. And don't stress about doing it... simply do it if and when you want to. Sleep when you're tired and wake up when you're rested. Simple, right? It is. But look how many challenges we create for ourselves by not doing it. Look at all the stress that comes from trying to outsmart our bodies rather than work with them. For what? We all know how good it feels going to bed on Friday night knowing that we get to sleep in on Saturday morning. It's wonderful. Even the thought of it makes us smile. So why don't we do it every night? Why don't we surrender to sleep when our body tells us, stay sleeping as long as it needs, and wake up when it naturally wants? Because it's not realistic, because it's not practical? Actually, it's very realistic, very practical, and what's more, it's very sensible. It took quite a story to convince us otherwise. Imagine going to bed every night with a feeling of abundance rather than scarcity. Imagine getting all the sleep you need and desire. How could that abundance not carry over into the rest of your day? Perhaps the resistance to this idea, writing it off because you think it is impossible, is indicative of how far you've actually strayed. Sure, you might have to make some other life changes in order to make it happen. But by changing the way you wake up, you might actually wake up.

2 – COLD SHOWER and/or POLAR PLUNGE after getting out of bed. Cold water is a game-changer. It wakes you up better than coffee or tea (not that I'm against either) and provides huge health benefits. It is a natural stimulant to the sympathetic nervous system: increases alertness, reduces inflammation, circulates blood and lymph, accelerates metabolism, enhances immune function, and speeds recovery. Cold water is a good spiritual practice: you can think about it all you want, you can stand in the shower with your hand on the knob, or dip your toe in the water in procrastination, but eventually, you get to turn off your mind and jump in. Cold showers get you funcomfortable first thing in the morning, reinforcing the daily habit of going outside your comfort zone, because that's where all the growth takes place. And if you don't have what it takes to practice being funcomfortable in the comfort of your own home, what business do you have being funcomfortable in front of a crowd? How will you lead others to grow if you can't lead yourself?

3 – HYDRATE. The solution to pollution is dilution. When you think you are hungry, drink some water first—the best water you can get, infused with fresh lemon. You might find, after drinking a liter or so, that you weren't actually hungry, only thirsty. If you do eat afterward, however, your digestion will be improved. Lemon has healthy enzymes, electrolytes, and Vitamin C, and helps alkalize the body. Chew your water. Drink it slowly, swish it in your mouth, mix it with saliva before swallowing it down. Drink water first thing in the morning, before eating breakfast, and drink plenty more throughout the day.

4 – SIT IN THE SUN, NAKED. Not only for the Vitamin D. Not only because it's funcomfortable. Not only because it increases healthy hormone production, gives you energy, and makes you grow. Do it because it feels good. Do it because it is your birthright. Find the balance between too much sun and too little sun.

*Bonus: GET GROUNDED while you're at it. Go barefoot in the grass, in the dirt, on the beach, etc. Shoes are great, but the shadow side is that they might separate us from the Earth's electric current. So go outside with your shoes off and see how your mood changes. Water, paradoxically, is also grounding. Walk through a creek, in the rain, or beneath a waterfall—not only will this ground you, it will flood you with mood enhancing negative ions. Maybe kids have so much energy and spirit because they run barefoot through the grass while playing with hoses and sprinklers…

5 – CONSCIOUSLY EAT local, organic, in-season foods with an attitude of gratitude for each ingredient and how it got to you. Take a moment to smell your food, look at your food, touch it, appreciate it, and pray for it. Maybe the degree to which you can be grateful for your food is the degree to which your food will be good for you. Know that what you are eating is turning into you, becoming a part of your body, providing fuel for your fire. Drink your food, and chew your water.

6 – FUNctional FITNESS. Key word, fun. Working out can be fun, so whatever that means to you, that's what I'd advise you to do. Sometimes I do it outside, in the sun, in the grass, doing whatever I feel like at 100% effort. Sprints, handstands, squats, pull-ups, dead hangs, etc. I get more done in seemingly less time, though in actuality time itself is flying by—because I am having fun. Other days I go to the gym, because that's what I feel like doing. Those days might be more "traditional" workouts, but I upgrade them by simultaneously listening to motivational speeches and mixes. It's a heightened sensory experience. Rather than only hearing the words, I feel them with my whole body, I absorb them into my mind, heart, muscles and lungs. Literally I am growing inside and out, strengthening inside and out, overcoming resistance externally while pushing myself internally.

*Listen to audio books while getting massages. If feels as if the words are being rubbed directly into you, allowing you to absorb more of what you're learning.

7 – TELL THE TRUTH. Practice being more honest in your daily life and relations. Use this phrase to get you over that hump of resistance: "I have something I want to share, but I observe that I'm nervous to do so." Typically, for me, that earns a thoughtful expression out of my listener, and they give me the floor.

8 – MEDITATE AND PRAY. Prayer is when you're speaking to God. Meditation is when you're listening to God. Recognize or experiment with the idea that whenever you are speaking you are praying, and whenever you are listening you are meditating. Everything you say is a prayer, and even if it seems like no one is listening, the Creator can hear every word. Conversely, whenever you are listening, listen closely, because God is telling you something.

9 – GET PAID to do the things you love to do, the things you would pay to do, and/or the things that you would continue to do regardless of whether you were getting paid to do them. Those things that make time and space disappear from consciousness are tied closely to your gift. You love to do them, and you give your love by doing them. Make the choice to live in that state of natural abundance which is unavoidable and everywhere you look. Make your "work" be something that fills you up, for that is the most sustainable "job" you can have.

10 – DO THESE EXERCISES. I've found that the best way to do these exercises is to conduct your own workshops for friends and family. First, give testimonials about how much you yourself have gotten out of these exercises. Second, extend the invitation for other people to join you. Invite them to invest time and money in something that you are willing to put on because of the results you yourself have gotten. Giving them the opportunity to invest money in the experience catalyzes them to get the value out of it. Third, take the lead and go first. If it's a confession exercise, you confess first. If it's the notice and imagine exercise, you go first. If it's the sharing judgments exercise, share your judgments. Lastly, team up with the people who seem most stoked by these ideas, to attract even more attractive people.